Sports
Illustrated

JOHN ELWAY

The Drive of a Champion

Stories excerpted from the
pages of *Sports Illustrated*

Original text by Michael Silver

SIMON & SCHUSTER

Simon & Schuster
Rockefeller Center
1230 Avenue of the Americas
New York, NY 10020

John Elway: The Drive of a Champion was produced by Bishop Books Inc., New York City.

Manufactured in the United States of America

10 9 8 7 6 5 4 3 2 1

Library of Congress Cataloging-in-Publication Data is available.

Cover photograph: Damian Strohmeyer
Back cover photograph: Peter Read Miller

ISBN: 0-684-85543-7

CONTENTS

INTRODUCTION

By *Michael Silver*

The waves broke, the mai-tais flowed and the sun dipped gently toward the warm Pacific Ocean, casting a soft reflection upon the surfers and sailboats and scantily clad vacationers along Waikiki Beach. It was just another lousy day in paradise, and then suddenly, a buzz infiltrated the warm Hawaiian breeze.

John Elway, the man of the moment, was in the house.

Five days after his victory in the greatest of Super Bowls, Elway, with Denver Broncos coach Mike Shanahan in tow, entered a beachfront bar and soaked up the Aloha spirit. He also indulged in a few other spirits, and deservedly so. In the wake of his triumphant performance against the Green Bay Packers in Super Bowl XXXII, a game it seemed everyone outside of Wisconsin wanted him to win, Elway was the toast of the Honolulu coast. He was a perpetual hug, a nonstop handslap—a living, breathing symbol of perseverance, determination and, best of all, redemption.

As Elway sat at a table with a group that included Shanahan and a pair of former NFL linemen, Ralph Tamm and Scott Adams, the legendary quarterback handled the onslaught of attention with politesse and poise. Besieged by a constant stream of

Early in his career Elway was beset by critics who questioned his looks, his character and his abilities.

5

well-wishers, Elway often paused in mid-story to receive slurred congratulations along the lines of, "That Super Bowl kicked ass, man. I won a lot of money on you guys." One sun-weathered, shirtless man pushed his way toward Elway, camera in hand, and panted, "Please, John, can you sign this? I used to be in the Beach Boys." An appropriate response would have been, "Yeah, right, and I play bass for the Rolling Stones." Instead, Elway smiled and said, "You guys are classic." And though Tamm and Adams admit that "we should have our pictures next to the word 'journeyman' in the dictionary," Elway existed comfortably as their equal. "I can't believe what a jerk you've become," Tamm told Elway, provoking a hearty stream of laughter as the sun went down.

Watching his easy, unentitled manner then—and, really, throughout the 1997 season, the 15th and most satisfying campaign of a career that will earn him a first-ballot induction to the Hall of Fame—it is difficult to believe that for so long Elway was portrayed as a spoiled prima donna, a silver-spoon-fed beach boy who pouted when he didn't get his way. To the contrary, virtually everyone who has played with Elway recently is struck by how utterly unaffected he is by fame, money and success.

How did America manage to be so wrong for so long? Partly, it was the package—blond hair, Southern California tan, toothy grin and muscular 6'3" frame. Then there was the pedigree, the fact that Elway, a coach's son, was as well prepared and as talented as anyone ever to take a snap from center. Finally, there was his manner of speaking, a valley-boy vernacular merged with an everyman honesty. Young John made no attempt to hide either his breezy confidence or the pain of his most stinging disappointments, such as Cal's miraculous, five-lateral kickoff return in 1982 that ended Elway's Stanford career, after which he accused the officials of ruining his last college game.

Upon turning pro, Elway had a choice to make: accept a big-money offer to play outfield for the New York Yankees or report to the Baltimore Colts, who had made him the

By the time Elway galloped into the '97 season, the world had come to appreciate his self-effacing style.

first pick of the NFL draft. The Colts' organization didn't appeal to Elway, who ultimately leveraged then-owner Robert Irsay into trading him to the Broncos. It was a lopsided deal that tilted the football landscape forever. The Colts, who promptly moved to Indianapolis, had only five winning seasons over the next 14 years, while the Broncos went on to play in four Super Bowls and win seven AFC Western Division titles during that span.

Still, because the expectations surrounding Elway were so lofty, he was often cited as much for what he didn't do as for what he actually accomplished.

Sure, he could throw a perfect spiral off the wrong foot and back across his body to the opposite sideline 40 yards downfield, but why couldn't he deliver the ball with more touch?

Granted, he could accept his niche as the biggest superstar not only in Denver but in the entire Rocky Mountain region, conducting himself admirably as a family man and auto dealer; but why couldn't Elway tip better, or give out tastier Halloween candy, or get along with his former coach, Dan Reeves?

Finally, while Elway entered the '97 season having won more games and having produced more fourth-quarter comebacks than any quarterback in NFL history, one question lingered: Why can't this great leader, a three-time Super Bowl loser, win the big one?

When Elway finally earned his ring in San Diego, guiding the Broncos to a thrilling, 31–24 upset of the Packers, all the stigmas vanished and seemed silly in retrospect. Regardless of his football future, he will go down as one of the greatest players in history, a champion who triumphed in the face of pressure and adversity.

More important, Elway, to those fortunate enough to have seen him play, will be remembered as a classy competitor, a man who danced in the stratosphere but never put on airs. From the shores of paradise to the peaks of Colorado, from the NFL trenches to the neighborhood taverns, this special athlete has finally received the appreciation he deserves.

Elway earned his legendary status in such classic contests as the '86 AFC title game (right).

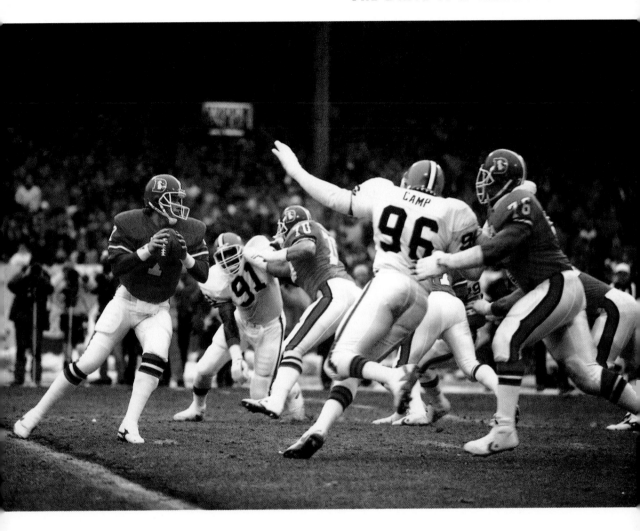

CLIMBING THE MOUNTAIN

CLIMBING THE MOUNTAIN

By Michael Silver

He can laugh about it now, a decade-and-a-half after the fact. But on Nov. 20, 1982, on a clear, crisp afternoon in Berkeley, California, John Elway felt as though the world was against him.

Elway's glorious career at Stanford had just ended in a most improbable manner. The archrival California Golden Bears had captured the Big Game with what would become known as The Play—a last-second, five-lateral kickoff return, the last 20 yards of which ran straight through the Stanford band.

The wildest finish in college football history was Elway's worst nightmare. Not only did it cost Stanford a berth in the Hall of Fame Bowl, but it also negated one of the greatest comebacks ever produced by the quarterback who would one day be the NFL's alltime comeback king. With a minute remaining, the wind swirling and the Cardinal trailing by two points, Stanford faced fourth-and-17 from its own 13-yard-line. Elway calmly stepped back into the pocket and unleashed the type of laser beam that only his arm can produce. Stanford receiver Emile Harry didn't so much catch the ball 29 yards downfield as assimilate it into his chest. Elway marched the Cardinal downfield to set up the 35-yard field goal that appeared to clinch the game.

A Stanford swimmer named Janet Buchan had a pretty good view of what happened on the ensuing kickoff. Along with a few other zealous Cardinal fans, she had followed the band onto the field when it appeared Cal's Dwight Garner had been downed before releasing a

Elway's days at Stanford produced a raft of NCAA records and the occasional epic victory.

lateral. Upon seeing the Bears' Kevin Moen charging toward the band with the ball, she recalls, "I had to turn around and run for dear life. It wasn't my finest hour." No matter: Elway ended up marrying her, anyway.

Five months after that game, as the NFL draft neared, America wasn't sure what to make of Elway. His father, San Jose State and future Stanford coach Jack Elway, wasn't the only one who viewed John as the greatest young quarterback prospect since Joe Namath. At Stanford, Elway would set five NCAA Division I records and produce the occasional epic victory, such as a triumph over No. 1-ranked Washington during his senior year. But Elway never led Stanford to a bowl game, and now, as the draft neared, he was threatening not to play pro football at all.

Elway had spent the summer after his junior year playing outfield for the New York Yankees' Class-A affiliate and was contemplating a big-money offer from owner George Steinbrenner. Partly, Elway wanted to leverage the Baltimore Colts, who had drafted him with the first overall selection, into trading him to a better-run franchise. But the idea of Elway playing baseball wasn't so far-fetched: During his six-week stint in Class-A ball, he hit .318, with 25 RBIs and no errors in 42 games.

Ultimately, Elway got what he wanted most: a trade to the Denver Broncos, where he was heralded as the organization's savior. There was resentment over his treatment of the Colts and pressure galore, and Elway took a while to blossom. He started 10 games as a rookie, threw twice as many interceptions as touchdowns and finished as the 17th-ranked passer in the 14-team AFC. Over the next two seasons he threw only two more touchdowns (40) than interceptions.

It wasn't until his fourth season, 1986, that Elway established his enduring greatness. After a brilliant regular-season campaign that earned him his first Pro Bowl appearance, Elway directed one of the classic comebacks in NFL playoff history. Trailing the Browns 20–13 with 5:32 remaining in the AFC title game, with a deafening din reverberating off the frozen dirt of Cleveland's Municipal Stadium, Elway engineered The Drive: a 98-yard march that sent the game into overtime. For an encore, he drove Denver 60 yards to set up Rich Karlis's game-winning field goal.

At 26, Elway was already a legend. Even when the Broncos stumbled in the Super Bowl, losing 39–20 to a New York Giants team with a dominant defense and an out-of-his-head quarterback in Phil Simms, it seemed only a matter of time before the football world would be his.

It wasn't until his fourth pro season and the legendary Drive that Elway staked his claim to greatness.

November 16, 1981

THE PHOENIX OF PALO ALTO

In 1980 Stanford's John Elway completed 65.4 percent of his passes, threw for 27 touchdowns and was named All-America—a rare distinction for a sophomore quarterback—as the Cardinal went 6—5. When the 1981 season began, hopes ran high in Palo Alto, but four straight losses to start the year brought the Cardinal thudding to earth. Still, as Sports Illustrated's Ron Fimrite recounted in his memorable profile of the rifle-armed quarterback, Elway had much to be proud of.

By Ron Fimrite

A marvelous paradox of this football season is that the college quarterback most prized by the pros plays for a team with one of the most god-awful records in the country. The quarterback is John Elway, and he throws bullet passes with cross-hair accuracy. The team is Stanford, which has been beaten [seven times].... Last Saturday's 63–9 victory over Oregon was only the second of the year for Stanford; on Oct. 10 the Cardinal squeaked by UCLA 26–23. Nevertheless, despite such massive insult and occasional injury—Elway has been bothered by a sprained right ankle, a chipped bone in his left hand and a mild concussion—the embattled young man has made the pros covet him all the more. In this hellish season he has thrown the ball 309 times and completed 175 passes for a .566 percentage and 2,202 yards. Fifteen of his passes have gone for touchdowns. That performance, following a ... season in which he completed 65.4% of 379 passes for 2,889 yards and 27 touchdowns [and became one of the handful of sophomore quarterbacks ever named All-America], has put him near the top of the quarterback heap at a school renowned for its passers....

From the neck up, Elway ... could be Andy Hardy, or Jody Baxter in *The Yearling*. His hair

Even in his earliest days at Stanford, Elway (right) attracted a lot of attention from the pro scouts.

falls like straw over an unlined forehead. His blue eyes are clear and his mouth, thick-lipped, is filled with alabaster teeth. That's the head. The rest of him is pure pro quarterback—lanky (6'4", 202), long-limbed, the chest of a weightlifter. Watching him fire his passes, reading about his record-shattering performances, one is likely to forget that this superman is, at 21, still a boy....

"I've learned a lot this year," Elway, ever cheerful, says. "You learn more from losing, I think.... It's a new situation for me—losing. It demonstrates how much the quarterback depends on the people around him...."

Stanford's dismal showing has in no way cooled the ardor professional scouts feel for the quarterback. "I've been in this business 20 years, and I'd have to say that Elway is the best I've ever seen," says Tony Razzano, director of college scouting for the 49ers.... "And sometimes when a player doesn't seem to have the accompaniment he might, you can't let it bother you that they're 2–7...."

The first week he stepped on a practice field as a freshman in 1979, Elway scared off two top quarterback prospects, Babe Laufenberg and Grayson Rogers, who quickly transferred to other schools ... where both have started at quarterback. Turk Schonert, a senior then, now with the Cincinnati Bengals, who had patiently waited his turn through

Elway's college sweetheart Janet Buchan (above) later became his wife; Elway's father Jack (right) had to face his son as an opponent.

the Guy Benjamin (49ers) and Steve Dils (Vikings) eras, was almost equally threatened by the freshman flamethrower. "Turk felt the pressure, no question," says [Stanford offensive coordinator Jim] Fassel. Schonert merely led the nation in passing that year. He almost had to in order to stave off Elway. "If you can play ahead of John Elway," says Fassel, "you're a great quarterback, and I don't care if you are a senior and he is only a freshman."

Andre Tyler, a brilliant Stanford split end...[says], "...most quarterbacks would not be physically able to even think about doing what Elway does routinely. You can be surrounded by defenders, and John will get the ball to you.... He throws so hard that it was a problem for us receivers at first.... For

a while the coaches debated whether to ask him to soften up. Finally they came to us and said, 'We're not going to ask John to change. It's up to you to adjust. He's our man....'"

With NFL scouts forming entire rooting sections and with big bucks being squirreled away to entice him, what could keep Elway from playing pro football? The New York Yankees could. The Yankees signed Elway to a ... contract [to play for their Class-A Oneonta (N.Y.) team next summer]....

For a youngster who spends most of his time throwing footballs, Elway is a remarkable baseball player....This past spring he hit .361 with nine homers and 50 RBIs in 49 games. In the NCAA Central Regionals he hit .444 and was voted onto the all-tournament team....

A lefthanded hitter with power, Elway is "made for Yankee Stadium," says Bill Bergesch, Yankee vice-president for baseball operations. "We project him as a superstar.

He's ... big and strong, he can run, he can hit and hit with power, and he's got that strong arm. We see him as our rightfielder down the road. Unfortunately, we are also aware that he has some talent in football...."

Elway's negotiator in his dealings with the Yankees and his closest confidant in all things is his father, Jack, 50. Theirs is a ... relationship abounding in mutual respect and admiration. It is a relationship marred, however, by an accident of fate: Jack Elway is the head football coach at San Jose State ... a traditional Stanford football opponent. The annual meetings between the ... teams are an excruciatingly painful experience for the entire Elway family, which includes wife-mother Janet and daughters-sisters Lee Ann and Jana [John's twin]....

"I tell people that my [recruiting] offer to John was $2,000 under the table, a new car and a mortgage on the house," [says Jack]. "I said I would go so far as to have an affair with his mother. Still, he didn't go for it.... I know that if I had said, 'John, come with me to San Jose,' he would've come, but that wouldn't have been fair to him. Still there are nights ... when I'll say to myself, 'Jack, old boy, you've got to be the dumbest sumbitch in this whole world. You had the best quarterback in America sitting across the breakfast table from you and you let him get away.'"

OH WHAT A NOTABLE VICTORY!

Elway's reputation preceded him throughout his impressive senior year at Stanford, so much so that he became the focus of every opponent's game plan. Stop Elway, the thinking went, and you stop Stanford. But such an approach could backfire, as No. 1-ranked Washington found out in 1982. Ron Fimrite observed how Elway's prodigious talents could drive teams to distraction.

By Ron Fimrite

It might just be possible, as the Washington Huskies learned to their considerable grief last Saturday, to have *too* much respect for John Elway.... The heavily-favored Huskies were so intent on stopping Elway, sometimes with suicidal safety blitzes, that they neglected, as Elway himself assuredly did not, the other weapons in the Cardinal arsenal.

The happy victory was based in large part on Elway's ability to handle the Washington blitz.

The oversight proved costly, as Stanford brought its record to 5–3 by beating Washington 43–31 in this season's biggest upset....

Elway [who completed 20 of 30 passes for 265 yards and two TDs] is one of those rare athletes [who so obsess] opponents that they tend to concentrate on him at the expense of all else.... Not without cause, of course. Elway already holds Pac-10 career records for completions (698), touchdown passes (72) and passing yardage (8,408), and he's only 26 yards shy of the conference's total offense standard of 8,178 yards.... But mere numbers cannot account for Elway's impact on opponents....

Halfway through the second quarter, on a first down from the Washington 46, the Huskies [leading 17–7] set up as usual to protect against the pass. Strong safety [Chris] O'Connor had moved in close to the line in a posture that indicated blitz. The safety blitz ... failed. Elway didn't pass. Instead, he handed off to halfback Mike Dotterer. [fullback Kaulana] Park, meanwhile, picked up the blitzing O'Connor and dropped him with a perfect block five yards behind the line of scrimmage, leaving a gaping hole in the defense. Now with O'Connor out of the action, Dotterer crossed the line of scrimmage and found open turf between him and the end zone....

Stanford again held Washington and forced another punt. Seven plays later Dotterer scored from one yard out and Stanford took the lead. Early in the third quarter [with Stanford up 24–17], Elway beat yet another Huskies safety blitz, this time with an 18-yard pass into the end zone to split end Emile Harry....

[Tight end Chris] Dressel, who had six catches for 106 yards, found himself free over the middle for most of the Washington game, partly because Elway was so effective at looking off the inside backers. "They were playing my eyes," said Elway. "By looking off, I got them flaring out. That left the middle open." At 8:17 of the third quarter [halfback Vincent] White ran around right end for a three-yard touchdown to give Stanford a 20-point lead that was soon shortened to 13....

It was left to 5' 8", 190-pound White to carry Stanford out of reach [with a 76-yard punt return with 5:30 remaining that was the second-longest in Stanford history]....

"If you told me we'd score 31 points and lose, I would be quite honest and say that would be a mistake," said [Huskies' coach Don] James.... "They read most of our blitzes real well," [he added], understating the case. "We were in a lot of coverage-type defenses and they did a great job of running against the package."

Obviously, a package designed specifically to stop Elway simply couldn't hold all the Cardinal players.

April 11, 1983

WOULD HE RATHER BE A UNITAS OR A MANTLE?

After finishing his college football career as a consensus All-America and Heisman Trophy runner-up, Elway sat back and watched the bidding war for his services. Despite Elway's not having played baseball at Stanford after his sophomore year, the negotiations took place on two fronts: the NFL and major league baseball. The Baltimore Colts had the first pick in the NFL draft, and the New York Yankees owned the baseball rights to Elway. As Sports Illustrated's Ralph Wiley reported, no matter which sport the 22-year-old chose, his prospects were bright.

By Ralph Wiley

The most desirable hunk of flesh to go on the scales in the professional sports marketplace in many a year is Stanford's 6'3", 205-pound John Elway ... [who will] be the No. 1 pick in the NFL draft on April 26. If he signs with a team in that league, it will undoubtedly be for the largest contract ever given an NFL rookie—possibly the largest ever given any NFL player. But Elway's a baseball player, too, with a longbow of an arm and a propensity for hitting fastballs on a line to distant places, and *those* talents could get him a contract commensurate with the size of George Steinbrenner's pocketbook.

The Yankees will make an all-out pitch for Elway's services late this week.... How high will they go? "The money isn't an issue," says Steinbrenner. "Never has been with us."

In the eyes of the prospective bidders, at least ... John the quarterback and John the outfielder appear to be about athletic equals. And he has done nothing to indicate that his liking for the two games is anything other than equal.

"I love to take two steps into a fly ball and then hum it home, just let it fly and watch it move," Elway says. "There's no feeling like that. But then, throwing a football is a tougher

Elway's enviable dilemma: Should he accept Steinbrenner's largesse or go for the gold in the NFL?

Elway's rifle arm and quick feet made him a sure-fire NFL No. 1 draft choice.

"We invited John to our Fort Lauderdale training camp last spring. He got into the batting cage for the first time, and [batting coach] Mickey Vernon told him to bunt one down the third-base line. He did. Told him to hit behind the runner, between first and second. He did. Same for second and third. Then he told him to hit it out of the park. He did."

NFL men are no less admiring.... Gil Brandt, the Dallas Cowboys' personnel chief, says if he had Joe Montana, Dan Fouts and Danny White on his team, he'd still pick Elway No. 1....

In the NFL the wooing of Elway begins with Frank Kush and Robert Irsay, the coach and owner, respectively, of the Baltimore Colts, the team with the No. 1 pick in the draft. Kush visited with Jack Elway in a restaurant near the San Jose State campus in February....

"[Kush] wanted to know how John felt about Baltimore," [says Jack]. "If John wanted to come, then he'd take him. If not, they'd trade the pick."

It now seems likely that the Colts will make that trade. John has never said publicly he won't play in Baltimore, but he admits he is cool to teams outside California, except the Seattle Seahawks—his girlfriend, Janet Buchan, a former All-America swimmer at Stanford, is from Tacoma—and the Cow-

release, a much harder thing to do.... I'll just let them all do the wheeling and dealing and then I'll decide," he says. "I know I can be happy either way. I won't look back...."

Says Steinbrenner, "I put an old scout, Dutch Dotterer, on John [Dotterer's grandson, Mike, was also a major league prospect, as an outfielder, and played in the same football backfield with Elway at Stanford]. Dutch reported he has an outstanding arm, is a fine defensive player, will hit with power and is a great competitor. He's rated a definite. I see a lot of Mickey Mantle in him.

boys. "I like California," he says. "I've never played in less than 45-degree weather...."

The intense interest in Elway among NFL teams exists despite a glut of quarterbacks in this year's draft.... Still available are Illinois' Tony Eason, Penn State's Todd Blackledge, Pitt's Dan Marino and Miami's Jim Kelly, all potential first-round choices....

If no deal is worked out between a team Elway favors and Elway himself before the draft, NFL insiders believe Elway will go with the Yankees.

And indeed he might decide to become a Yankee, for the sheer challenge of it. He believes he could do fine in the major

leagues, despite that bane of the phenom, the breaking pitch. "I'm not going to say I can't hit it," Elway says. "It might take two or three years to get to the big leagues, but I think I could."

Says Jack, "John felt that pressure of playing for money in Oneonta [the Yankees' Class-A farm team]. He slumped, and he called me and said, 'Dad, I think my goal is to hit .100.' I told him to be aware of his mistakes but not to let them crush him." Elway found his swing, finishing the six-week tour by hitting .356 in July and .318 overall, with 25 RBIs and no errors in 42 games.

"The Yankees have been extremely good to John," says [Elway's agent Marvin] Demoff, "but they must be aware that he would be passing up a tremendous opportunity. In football, he could be the best player ever at the most dominant position in the game...."

Jack insists he doesn't care which sport his son chooses. "I just want him to be excited, and dollars won't decide that," says Jack. "You can't be great playing on a dollar basis. You've got to have your heart and soul in it.... I'd feel real successful if I could just preserve for John the joy of playing ball. Because that's where he'll find his greatness."

Elway's accurate arm and ability to go deep made him a coveted baseball prospect too.

August 15, 1983

In Denver, Delirium is Spelled E-L-W-A-Y

Elwaymania seized Denver on May 2, 1983 with the signing of the prized quarterback to a five-year, $5 million deal. Nearly 54,000 fans poured into Mile High Stadium for Elway's professional debut on Aug. 5, a preseason game against Seattle. Broncos fans welcomed their savior and, as Sports Illustrated's Douglas S. Looney observed, he delivered.

By Douglas S. Looney

In a show-stopping performance that blazed across the Denver sky last Friday night, Bronco quarterback John Elway established himself—in exactly four minutes, 22 seconds—as a phenom of extraordinary proportions. That's how long it took the NFL's most heralded rookie in eons, and at $1 million a year its highest-paid

Elway had good reason to smile after his stunning debut performance in a Broncos uniform.

player, to grab the Broncos—2–7 last year and trailing in this game 7–3—by the throat and march them, nay, stampede them, 75 yards into the Seattle end zone for the winning touchdown. The drive took 10 plays—Elway's first 10 as a pro—and during it the quarterback completed five of six passes, in the rain.

If he keeps this up, he'll be a legend by September and eligible for sainthood by October. Pete Rozelle instructs us to call them preseason games, not exhibitions. But make no mistake. This was an exhibition. Of greatness. Of talent that has not come the NFL's way since Joe Namath....

Elway played only in the second half, after veteran Steve DeBerg, the Broncos' regular quarterback last season, went the first 30 minutes. The fans booed DeBerg when he was introduced, and, as it turned out, that was the high point of his night. Once during the second half Elway went to the sidelines for two plays because of problems with the tape on his shoes, and DeBerg replaced him. The rowdy Bronco locos were beside themselves with boos. It wasn't fair, it wasn't decent—but it was to the point....

Of course, Elway got the game ball. Of course, his passing percentage (.667) on 10–of–15 was impressive. Of course, he later praised his teammates. And, of course, he said,

"I've got a long way to go, and a lot to learn...."

Said Bronco coach Dan Reeves: "He did not execute all the plays well but he did a good job overall." But Reeves's demeanor belied his restraint; the coach looked like a man who had turned on his lawn sprinkler and found it was spewing oil. The next day it was announced that Reeves had agreed to a four-year extension to his contract....

Elway—hounded and besieged every step by fans and media—is the first able-bodied young quarterback the Broncos have ever had. And only three out of the Broncos' list of 30 have been any good at all. First, there was old and creaky Frank Tripucka, who led them to their first break-even season, 7–7 in 1962 in the old AFL. And there was old and creaky Charley Johnson, who guided them to their first-ever winning season, 7-5-2 in 1973. And then there was old and creaky Craig Morton, who took them to the Super Bowl in 1977. That's it....

The situation was summed up best and most succinctly after the game had ended when Bronco kicker Rich Karlis ... walked up to [Broncos owner Edgar] Kaiser, shook hands and said to the boss, "Nice acquisition." Nobody had to ask which nice acquisition Karlis was talking about. That's the way it is when you are dealing with a phenom going on legend going on saint.

GETTING THERE THE HARD WAY

Now simply referred to as The Drive, the first installment in the Elway legend came in the 1986 AFC championship game against Cleveland. Trailing by seven points with 5:32 remaining, Elway engineered a heart-stopping 98-yard march to tie the Browns with 37 seconds left, then moved them into position for the field goal in OT that put the Broncos in the Super Bowl. Sports Illustrated's Rick Telander was there to report the miracle.

By Rick Telander

Have you ever been mean to a nice old dog? Did you sit there with a tail-wagging mongrel at your knee and kindly offer him a meaty bone, hold it barely in front of the pooch's eager snout and at the last instant, just after his head lunged forward but before his teeth clicked shut, pull the bone away?..

Then you've been John Elway ... who yanked the bone from the mouth of the Cleveland Dawgs, er, Browns, 23–20 in overtime, for the AFC Championship before 79,915 stunned fans in Cleveland Stadium on Sunday....

The game was over. The Browns had won and the Broncos had lost. It was that simple. But then, with 5:32 remaining and Denver trailing 20–13, Elway led his team 98 yards down the field on as dramatic a game-saving drive as you'll ever see....

Playing on unfriendly turf, generating offense where there had been precious little before, Elway ran, passed, coaxed and exhorted his team in magnificent style. Finally, with 39 seconds left and the ball on the Browns' five-yard line, he found Mark Jackson slanting over the middle in the end zone and hit him with a touchdown bullet. After that, the overtime was a mere formality. Elway took the Broncos 60 yards this time, giving Rich Karlis field goal position at the Cleveland 15-yard line and a sweet piece of advice: "It's like prac-

Elway's performance in The Drive left little doubt about his credentials for greatness.

tice." Karlis's 33-yard field goal, his third of the afternoon, cut through the Browns like a knife.

Only a few minutes earlier, back in regulation, when the home team still had that big seven-point lead, nobody in the delirious Cleveland throng could have imagined such a nightmarish turn of events. Browns wide receiver Brian Brennan had just made it 20–13 by twisting safety Dennis Smith into a bow tie on a 48-yard touchdown reception from quarterback Bernie Kosar, a play that seemed destined to go straight into the NFL archives....

The Broncos misplayed Mark Moseley's ensuing knuckleball kickoff and downed it at their own two-yard line. There was no way they were going to drive 98 yards and score a touchdown. No way. On its two previous fourth-quarter possessions Denver had moved just nine and six yards, respectively....

To make matters infinitely worse, Elway had a bad left ankle, and the Browns had a ferocious, yapping defense. And straight behind them was the Dawg Pound, the east end-zone section where fans ... bellowed for their Dawgs to treat Denver like a fire hydrant. Even from this distance the Broncos were amazed at the insane howling of the Pound....

It didn't matter. Using hand signals and a silent count, Elway began moving his team....

"In the huddle after that kickoff to the two he smiled—I couldn't believe it—and he said, 'If you work hard, good things are going to happen,'" says wide receiver Steve Watson. "And then he smiled again...."

The game was on the line. The season, too. Elway completed a short pass to Sammy Winder. Three plays later he broke from the pocket and ran for 11 yards and a first down. He sent a 22-yarder to Steve Sewell and followed with one for 12 yards to Watson. Three plays, three first downs and all of a sudden Denver had the ball on Cleveland's 40-yard line with 1:59 to go....

But not so fast. After an incompletion on first down and an eight-yard sack on second, Denver had to call timeout. Third-and-long ... Watson went in motion ... and the snap deflected off him—three crucial plays, three crucial miscues—but Elway saved the day by getting control of the ball and passing 20 yards to Jackson for a first down at the Browns' 28.

Elway had entered the magic realm that few athletes enter. He was doing whatever he wanted. "We shut him down the whole game," said Browns defensive end Sam Clancy afterward, "and then in the last minutes he showed what he was made of...."

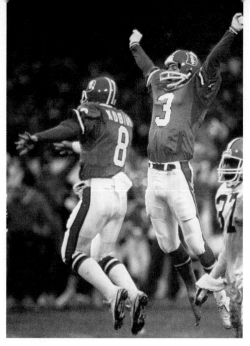

Elway (above) drilled a pair of strikes in OT to set up the winning field goal by Karlis (right).

Denver was approaching the goal line and the awesome din of the Dawg Pound. Biscuits thrown by fans coated that part of the field. "You could feel the things crunching under your feet when you ran," said receiver Vance Johnson....

A 14-yard pass to Sewell put the ball on the 14 and, after an incompletion, Elway broke cover and rushed for nine yards to the five. On third-and-one with 39 seconds left, he delivered the crusher. Dropping back, he fired a rocket to Jackson angling across from the left side into the end zone. "They were in a zone and the corner let Mark go,"

said Elway. "I tried to put it in the hole."

In the process, he nearly drilled a hole in Jackson's belly. "I felt like a baseball catcher," the 174-pound receiver said later. "That was a John Elway fastball, outside and low."

It was a touchdown, and after the extra point the score was tied 20–20. The drive, one of the finest ever engineered in a championship game, had been performed directly in the Browns' faces.... One was left with the distinct feeling that Elway would have marched his team down a 200-yard- or 300-yard- or five-mile-long field to pay dirt....

January 26, 1987

TOUGH GUY IN THE CLUTCH

As the Broncos prepared to meet the heavily-favored Giants in Elway's first Super Bowl appearance, the quarterback took time out with Rick Telander to reflect on subjects ranging from his upbringing to his public image to the already-famous Drive the previous week against the Browns. One week later Elway would suffer the first of his three Super Bowl losses as the Giants rolled to victory, 39—20. Elway would not forget the experience.

By Rick Telander

As a former Bishop of Baltimore, I have come to admire the choice John Elway made.

J. FRANCIS STAFFORD
Archbishop of Denver

Thank you, Your Excellency. We would expect as much from a man whose business is forgiveness and who, not coincidentally, happens to root for the Denver Broncos.

But what about those hard-luck Baltimoreans who felt that John Elway ... had spat on their city when he said he would rather play minor league baseball than pro football in Baltimore? The Colts took his threat seriously. They chose Elway first in the 1983 draft, then traded him to Denver for tackle Chris Hinton, backup quarterback Mark Herrmann and Denver's first-round pick in 1984.... A lot of people resented Elway for forcing the Colts' hand.

"Baltimore," says Elway now, addressing the entire city from a stool in the Broncos' locker room, "I'm sorry.... I never should have said I wouldn't play in Baltimore.... What I meant was the Colts' *organization*.... I had nothing against the city. I just didn't want to play for the owner, Robert Irsay, or the coach, Frank Kush. Kush was a military type. I wouldn't even take a recruiting trip to Arizona State when he was the coach there...."

Elway is genuinely pained by the way he has been perceived since entering the NFL,

The toothy grin sometimes irked his critics, but Elway has smiled all the way to four Super Bowls.

Through the years, Elway learned to cope with a life spent in the media spotlight.

and … he would love to do some image polishing. "I hope people can get to know what I'm really like," he says. "I have the image of being a spoiled brat, and I *hate* it."

What he really is, says Elway, is "a private, fun-loving, family man." He and wife Janet have one child, 14-month-old Jessica, and another baby is due this spring.

The Broncos quarterback was hurt in the beginning by comments by such critics as former Steeler quarterback Terry Bradshaw ("He ought to grow up and pay his dues") and a sort of vague public impression that Elway just *looked* like a smart aleck. He had that blond hair and those big white teeth, and he always seemed to be half-smiling. Some people were irritated by his too-good-to-be-true background.…

Furthermore, Elway's five-year $5 million contract made him the highest-paid player in the NFL—and a lot of people were eager to see him fail.

At first, they got their wish.…

[In his first] season Elway finished as the 17th-rated passer in the 14-member AFC. He showed moments of genius along the way … but mostly he just looked bewildered.

"He wasn't ready," says Reeves. "The biggest problem was the language. It was like somebody learning Spanish and passing all the classroom tests and then going to Mexico, and all of a sudden it's coming at you so fast, you don't know what's going on.…"

And the failing nearly unhinged Elway. "All of a sudden there were no weaknesses on defense," he says, thinking back. "In college, 15-yard cushions on receivers are common. But in the pros, unless the other team blows a coverage, nobody is going to be wide open.…"

There is a stack of mail by Elway's stool, and he picks up an envelope and opens it. It's a telegram from George Raveling, the basketball coach at USC. From sixth to ninth grade Elway, who was born in Port Angeles, Wash., attended Raveling's summer camp at Washington State.… The telegram reads: *Dear Shotgun: Congratulations on your great season. Best of luck in the Super Bowl. I still think you should have played basketball.…*

only 79.0, 11th-best in the NFL. In the play-offs his rating is a lowly 65.2 (50% completion rate, two touchdowns, three interceptions), while Broncos opponents have a 90.8 rating. But guess who's going to the Super Bowl.

"I have no idea why we have to wait so long to get going," says Elway in genuine dismay.... "I think what happens to me is that in tight situations I stop worrying about turnovers. There is no pressure. I can just cut it loose...."

The other factor, of course, is that Elway can run. Indeed, he started his football career as a running back in the fifth grade.... "I was always the fastest kid in my class," [he recalls]. "Then in the seventh grade I started growing and my speed went. That's when I became a quarterback."

At Stanford, Elway had to sprint for his life. With the Broncos he loves to run, to make other teams miss and pound the turf in disgust. He is Denver's alltime leader for backs in average gain per carry (4.8), and he has led AFC quarterbacks in rushing for the last three years—stats he is most proud of....

The quarterback knows that the Broncos aren't given much of a chance in the coming game, but that is almost soothing to him. "Being an underdog means nothing to us," says Elway. "There's no pressure. We have everything to gain and nothing to lose."

Let the two-minute drill begin.

At home, Elway's daughter Jessica helped him keep the game in perspective.

Clearly, though, he has chosen the right sport. The way he engineered "the Drive" ... is proof enough of that....

Indeed, the Drive confirmed that Elway is, with Dan Marino, one of the two best come-from-behind QBs in the game. Elway has never produced the sparkling across-the-board stats of other premier NFL quarterbacks, mainly because he doesn't get fired up until the game is on the line.... This year he completed 55.6% of his passes for 3,485 yards and 19 TDs, but his quarterback rating was

NEARING THE SUMMIT

NEARING THE SUMMIT

By Michael Silver

For 15 precious minutes of football, on a balmy January afternoon in San Diego, it looked like the California golden boy would have his day in the sun.

On the Broncos' first offensive play of Super Bowl XXII, John Elway dropped back to pass and fired a 56-yard bomb to Ricky Nattiel. Touchdown, Denver. The Broncos got the ball back and Elway pitched the ball to halfback Steve Sewell, raced across the line of scrimmage and *caught* a 23-yard pass, setting up a field goal. It was Denver 10, Washington 0, and it looked like another Super Bowl blowout was unfolding.

The rout was on, alright: Led by Redskins quarterback Doug Williams, who had a career day, and a halfback named Timmy Smith, who was the ultimate one-hit wonder, Washington rolled off 35 points in the second quarter and cruised to a 42–10 victory. It was the Broncos' second consecutive Super Bowl defeat, and this time Elway, who completed only 14 of 38 passes, was shouldering some of the blame. Never mind that, as usual, Denver had climbed within spitting distance of the summit on Elway's back. The Broncos' other 10 offensive starters that day were selected to a grand total of four Pro Bowls during their careers—two apiece for halfback Sammy Winder and guard Keith Bishop, neither of whom will ever receive a Hall of Fame vote.

Two years later, in January 1990, Elway led Denver to its third Super Bowl in four years. As in the previous two AFC title runs, he faced the Browns in the conference championship

Elway's greatness was now established, but he still lacked the ultimate credential: a Super Bowl win.

game and played brilliantly. And then, once again, Elway fizzled in the Super Bowl. This time, he met up with perhaps the only quarterback of his era who would rival him for overall excellence and grace under fire: San Francisco's Joe Montana, who had already led the 49ers to three Super Bowl triumphs. These 49ers were one of history's greatest teams, and the Broncos never had a chance. San Francisco rolled to a 55–10 victory, intercepting Elway twice and limiting him to 108 passing yards.

Those losses made Elway a symbol of big-game futility. But he had other problems as well. In Denver, media coverage of Elway bordered on the absurd. One article questioned the choice of Halloween candy his family disbursed. Another suggested he was a lousy tipper at restaurants. People made fun of his hair, his wobbly gait, his teeth. Washout linebacker Brian Bosworth, of all people, said Elway "looks like Mr. Ed." More jokes cropped up after the infamous police chase involving O.J. Simpson in 1994: *O.J. was driving a slow, white Bronco. Like Elway. Get it?*

By 1991, Elway's relationship with Broncos coach Dan Reeves had become strained. Their conflict stemmed partly from Reeves's football philosophy—a conservative style that Elway felt denied him the opportunity to optimize his talents—and partly from a personality clash. Mike Shanahan, the Broncos' talented offensive coordinator, served as a buffer between the two men. In '91, the Broncos went 12–4 and won their fifth AFC West title of the Elway Era, then faced the Houston Oilers in an AFC divisional playoff game. The Broncos trailed 24–23 when they got the ball on their own 2-yard line with 2:07 remaining. Elway, engineer of The Drive in Cleveland five years earlier, put forth the best sequel since *The Godfather, Part II*, converting a pair of fourth downs and setting up David Treadwell's game-winning, 28-yard field goal.

But the Broncos lost the AFC title game to Buffalo, with Elway leaving after three quarters due to a thigh injury. Then the pain got worse: Reeves fired Shanahan, Elway bristled, and the Broncos fell to 8–8 the following season. Reeves was fired and replaced by Wade Phillips, but Denver played in just one playoff game over the next two seasons, and Phillips was axed as well.

Finally, in January 1995, Elway got his wish: Shanahan, his friend and mentor, took over as the Broncos' head coach. It took Elway a full season to adapt to Shanahan's new offensive system, which had been influenced by the coach's stint as the 49ers' offensive coordinator. But once he did, Elway felt like a quarterback reborn.

In his second Super Bowl Elway and the Broncos were laid low by the Redskins' onslaught.

GUNFIGHT AT MILE HIGH CORRAL

The Broncos rebounded from their crushing loss in Super Bowl XXI to win a second straight AFC West crown, going 10-4-1 in the strike-shortened 1987 season. Sports Illustrated's Rick Reilly was on hand for Denver's first-round playoff victory over the tough-talking Houston Oilers, which set up a Broncos—Browns rematch for the AFC title.

By Rick Reilly

Nobody, not even the Italians, has ever made a more low-rent, late-night, shoot-'em-up, leave-at-intermission, B Western than Sunday's Houston–Denver playoff game at Mile High Stadium. Too bad it was a 34–10 walkout rout by the Broncos, because the casting was terrific.

You had Denver quarterback John Elway as the Duke, firing bullets and walking that walk, that swagger of a man who just rode in from Amarillo on a saddle two sizes too small.

And you had the Duke's trusty sidekick wide receivers, the Three Amigos, talking that talk, catching the Duke's bullets in their teeth, phoning their agents. Led by "the Vance" (never just Vance) Johnson, who will wear any of 30 different hair colors—the Boz starter set—the Amigos write messages to beaten cornerbacks on the soles of their shoes, such as BYE-BYE and ADIOS.

There was even a bad guy dressed in black, the Houston Oilers' own Johnny Cash, head coach Jerry Glanville, whose sartorial selections make him a real honest-to-goodness confidant of Cash himself. Cash sends Glanville black jackets and black sunglasses and letters addressed to "the Coach in Black" from "the Man in Black." Could we make this up? Cash must like the way Glanville walks the line.

Not so for the orange-skinned faithful in Denver, who figured Glanville went over the line before the game when he said, "This is just the second stop on a four-game schedule. We're going to San Diego." And then there was this: "If it snows, tell [the Broncos] to wear

Elway, a.k.a. the Duke, loaded the Broncos on his stagecoach and drove them past Houston.

43

Elway's cross-field bullet was snared by Kay in the end zone, putting the Broncos in front 24–3.

snowshoes, 'cause we're going to run right around them."

So who was snowing whom? Houston, the boys in the bubble, hadn't played outside a dome since Nov. 15, and now they were heading to some of the country's most out-of-control air-conditioning. The Broncos had the best record in the AFC, had won 27 of their last regular-season 32 in their own corral and had Elway, the AP NFL MVP. O.K.? To Broncomaniacs, Glanville's were fightin' words.

Didn't bother Jerry. He figured his hand was as good as any in this game....

Unfortunately, before we could get much past the opening theme music—and long before the big gunfight scene—the Oilers went and plugged themselves full of lead.

With Houston backed up at its own four-yard line, on its second snap of the game, Glanville got this genius idea to try an end zone, overhand lateral to running back Mike Rozier on the far sideline, a play Houston calls Stagger Lee. Why throw a lateral to the man with the stoniest hands on the club, in your own end zone, so early in the biggest game that the franchise has had in eight years, on the road, in one of the most unforgiving stadiums in the country? That's one for Glanville to think about. What happened is that the ball hit Rozier in the numbers and the hands before bouncing stagger-ly into the arms of Bronco Steve Wilson at the one-yard line.

Package for Mr. Elway! Package for Mr. Elway!

It took Denver two plays to score. "Just love those one-yard drives," said Elway....

Maybe the show wasn't over right then, but you could almost see the credits rolling. The young Oilers were a group therapy session after that, all dangling nerve ends. They were called for 10 penalties on the day, three in one Denver series. It was on Houston's next possession that Rozier fumbled, and after that [quarterback Warren] Moon seemed flustered. On the ensuing drive, he made an all-mallard pass, a ball that looked like it was clinging to breakfast jelly on his fingers before fluttering off and into the hands of Denver linebacker Karl Mecklenburg. Six plays later, Elway found tight end Clarence Kay's fingertips for a 27-yard touchdown. Two Houston turnovers, 14 Denver points. A minute and a half left in the first quarter. Here's your hat. What's your hurry?

The rest was not pretty. After swapped field goals, the Duke found the Vance for 55 yards on a broken play. It wasn't a touchdown, but close enough, so Johnson gave the crowd his best flamenco dancer olé, which is also what the Vance wants fans to holler anytime one of the Amigos catches a pass....

Soon after the Vance dance, Elway was rolling right from the Houston one, not finding anybody open and about to be thumped, when he suddenly threw *left*, across Oiler helmets and into the six-point hands of Kay. See ya, Blue. Make it 24–3.

And make it just another piece of True Grit from Elway, a man who will never give you stats that do a triple somersault out of your newspaper (Sunday: 14 for 25, 259 yards, two touchdowns throwing, one running), but who constantly gives you plays that make you check your eyeglass prescription. If the Broncos become the seventh team to return to the Super Bowl after having played in the previous one, they will have done it riding the Duke's stagecoach....

Perhaps next year our coach in black will get his shot....

On this day, [though], as the sun settled slowly in the west, there were only Glanville's hollow words, his glum face and a cruel sign that rose amid the hooting Mile High swarms.

It said: JERRY, CAN I HAVE THOSE SAN DIEGO TICKETS?

January 25, 1988

HIGH AND MIGHTY

The Broncos and the Browns met again for the AFC title, but this time nearly everything was reversed from the previous year's classic: Now Denver was at home and desperately defending a late lead. Now it was Cleveland quarterback Bernie Kosar who couldn't miss as he led his team to what seemed the inevitable tying touchdown. But as Rick Reilly reported, there was one constant from the '87 meeting: a crushing, late-game blow for the Browns.

By Rick Reilly

They say the one thing you learn from history is that you do not learn at all. It must be true, because history keeps rising up to clobber the Cleveland Browns. Three times in this decade the Browns have come within a minute of winning playoff games and three times that minute has turned into an entire off-season. First, there was the interception Brian Sipe served up to the Raiders in their divisional playoff game in 1980. Then there was John Elway's Sunday Drive for the AFC title a year ago. But who could have seen this one coming? This time, again within a few ticks of a Super Bowl berth, the Browns stayed highlight reel for highlight reel with Elway. And they held up under a din that threatened to crack the foundation of Mile High Stadium.

What they didn't count on was an unknown cornerback with a hero complex.

What they didn't count on was Jeremiah Castille, cut adrift by the Tampa Bay Buccaneers before this strange season began, sitting there on the Denver bench for much of the long afternoon and into the night. He had watched John Elway direct the Broncos to a 21–3 halftime lead, with poster-perfect passes and Fred Astaire feet. He had watched Bernie Kosar drag the Browns back to within a touchdown, 38–31, using shot-put heaves for passes and a running style that might suggest bunion problems. He had watched a parade of famous, rich men pass

Elway's Fred Astaire feet helped the Broncos waltz to a 21–3 halftime lead over Cleveland.

46

in front of him and didn't feel like he belonged with any of them....

Suddenly, his chance came. Filling in for starting cornerback Steve Wilson, who had aggravated a leg injury, Castille found himself one of the 11 Broncos who were backpedaling down the field at Kosar's whim as the clock wound down. The Browns needed a touchdown to send the game into overtime, and the way Kosar was playing, that seemed inevitable. After all, the Browns had scored TDs on their first four possessions of the second half and had stomped from their own 25 to the Denver eight in less than three minutes on this little tour. What was going to stop them—City of Denver snowplows?

And so, on second-and-five from the eight, Kosar handed the ball to his 215-pound running back, Earnest Byner, who, finding the middle clogged, broke left, picked up speed and encountered a nearly unobstructed view of the goal line. "I knew we needed a big play," Castille said afterward. "This was a money game." Sure, but did this game have room for another hero?

Didn't this show already belong to Elway and Kosar, the yin and yang of the NFL? Talk about strange casting, how did these two ever end up on the same stage—the AFC title game—two years in a row? If you

Foreshadowing his later heroics, Castille (28) stripped Webster Slaughter in the fourth quarter.

stood them next to each other on a beach, Kosar would look like "Before" to Elway's "After." Elway is muscular. Kosar is built like a CPA whose health club membership has expired. Elway is beach-boy blond. Kosar looks like a mattress salesman. Elway's throwing motion would make Koufax envious. Kosar throws, as Jim Murray of the *Los Angeles Times* once wrote, "like a guy losing a bar of soap in the shower." Elway's passes arrive so angrily they leave marks on receivers' palms. You could catch Kosar's passes with a beer in each hand....

After throwing an interception on, yes, the first possession, Kosar got it there Sunday with astonishing precision. "It was like 'ugly, ugly, ugly, great play,'" said Broncos linebacker Ricky Hunley. "He was *hot*."

So hot was Bernie that, as he watched Byner make the turn on that fateful run, he was only eight yards away from possibly erasing memories of the Drive—the 98-yard minor miracle Elway pulled off in Cleveland last year to win a trip to the Super Bowl....

Maybe the only man in the Mountain time zone who wasn't thinking overtime was Castille. Two plays before, Byner had gained six yards, but Castille had come back to the huddle to tell his teammates, "I almost got the ball loose." Now Byner was headed toward the end zone, an arm's length from Castille, who reached out his left arm, trying to strip Byner of the ball. "I just felt like he was in such a position that it wouldn't have done me any good to make the tackle. He was going to score. I had to try and strip it. That's all I had left."

Byner landed in the end zone. Unfortunately, the ball didn't make the trip with him. Castille, who had dislodged it, fell on it at the three, and, after a long pileup,

emerged with his prize.

Denver took a deliberate safety with eight seconds left in order to kick out of harm's way, and won it 38–33, thus earning a third trip to the Super Bowl and becoming the first team since the 1978–79 Pittsburgh Steelers to repeat as AFC champions....

The Denver defense kept Kevin Mack and the Cleveland running game largely in check.

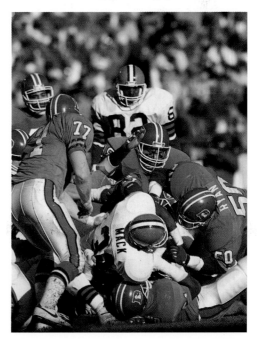

November 6, 1989

'I'M ABOUT TO SUFFOCATE'

Following a substandard 1988 season in which he threw 19 interceptions and the Broncos missed the playoffs with an 8–8 record, Elway discovered how fickle demanding fans such as Denver's could be. Rick Reilly talked with Elway about the increasing media and public scrutiny he faced in his seventh year, even though his team was 6–2 and atop the AFC West.

By Rick Reilly

Them thar hills of Colorado are full of happy campers this time of year, but Denver Bronco quarterback John Elway is not one of them. Everywhere he goes, he's the roast of the town. "They talk about my hair," he says. "They talk about my teeth, how much I tip, how much I drink, how I'm playing, when I'll talk to the media. I'm sick of it."

In his seventh year in Denver, Elway is starting to itch. He says he feels like a big fish in a very small pond. "And I'm running out of water," he says. "I'm about to suffocate."

With Elway's poor season last year—he ranked 18th among NFL quarterbacks—and his erratic first half in '89, some people, even outside Denver, have been trying to saw the legs off his throne. Before the Eagles defeated the Broncos on Sunday, 28–24, Philadelphia coach Buddy Ryan said what some folks have been thinking—that Elway is not the shiniest model on the showroom floor anymore. "People used to compare Randall Cunningham to John Elway," said Ryan. "Now they compare Elway to Randall."

Elway could only shrug at the remark. "Just another day in Beat Up John Elway Week," he said.

What's wrong with this picture is that Elway's team has been kicking gluteus for most of this year. Despite losing to Philly, the Broncos are 6–2 and two games up on the rest of the AFC West....

Elway's day Sunday was almost as schizophrenic as his season—overthrowing wide-open

The intense fan and media scrutiny had Elway feeling pursued off the field as well as on it.

50

receivers by five yards one moment, then dropping a spiral, sidearm, over the fingernails of two Eagles and into the arms of some stunned Bronco the next. He had 19 completions, 20 misses, eight overthrows, three flagrantly wide balls, two drops, three interceptions, four miracles, seven sacks, two TDs by air, one by land, and 278 yards—all while wearing the Eagle pass rush like an overcoat.

But if Elway is this unhappy at 6–2, imagine what he would be like at 2–6. "I don't want to sound like a crybaby, so I don't talk about it," he says. "But it's just gotten to be too much lately. I'm just torn up inside right now."

Would he like to be traded? "I don't know." Would he like to quit? "I don't know." How much more is he willing to take? "Not much." Would he like to pull a Steve Carlton and not talk? "Yeah, but nobody in this organization would let me do it." Would he like to leave town? "We bought a place in Palm Springs, and we're going to get away more often now."

This is a guy who is 60-30-1 as a starter; among active quarterbacks, only San Francisco's Joe Montana has won more games. However, the stats don't stop there. They also show that he ranks 24th this season among NFL quarterbacks. That he has thrown for 200 or more yards only three times this year. (He did it 10 times last season.) That he has only nine touchdown

passes in '89, along with 11 interceptions, and has completed only 50.4% of his throws, down from his career percentage of 54.3.

All of which leads us to another problem. To Bronco fans, Ferraris don't blow gaskets and Elways don't have bad years, so they hunt for character flaws. "Just because I don't have the numbers this year, they start talking about the other stuff," he says. Some of the shots get pretty cheap.

Teeth: Too big. A remark made famous by the Seattle Seahawks' bad-boy linebacker Brian Bosworth—"Elway looks like Mr. Ed"—has stuck among the Elway-haters in town.

Hair: Too long. Though it's not as long as wide receiver Vance Johnson's, whose ponytail has to be bound up twice and tucked into his helmet.

Tips: Too small. Columnist Teri Thompson of the *Rocky Mountain News* wrote last week that Elway "never tips waitpeople." O.K., one writer remembers Elway having five 99-cent beers and leaving the pennies as the tip. But that was six years ago. A few weeks back in Cleveland, Elway left a $10 bill on a $30 check. Journalism marches on.

Media relations: Not accessible enough. During lunch breaks at practice he sometimes hides in a trainer's room and plays cards. After workouts he'll occasionally walk back to the players' building via the street

outside the training complex rather than face the hordes waiting for him on the grounds.

Drinking: Rumors abound in Denver that Elway has a drinking problem, but he has never been arrested for driving under the influence, has never been picked up on any charge by local police, has never worn a Betty Ford Center T-shirt. What fertilizes the rumors are the town's two Bronco-bitten newspapers and four omnivorous sports talk shows on TV. A *Rocky Mountain News* gossip columnist even wrote last week, "John Elway was spotted at Rodney's playing backgammon and drinking Bud Lights."

One positive in '89 was the return of Mike Shanahan (top, right) as quarterbacks coach.

Says Elway, "I think I'm going to sue. Those were Coors Lights...."

Passes: Too few. It's true that Elway's numbers are down, but so are his chances to throw. The Broncos have passed 40 fewer times than at the same point last season, and they're running more....

"The frustrating thing is," says Elway, "as good as we are on defense, I know we've got a chance to win it all if we can just get that good on offense."

Translation: Palm Springs can wait.

January 22, 1990

ONCE MORE ... WITH FEELING

Elway overcame his skirmishes with the Denver media to lead the Broncos to an 11–5 record and a fourth AFC West title during his tenure. After beating Pittsburgh in the divisional playoffs, Denver met Cleveland in the AFC championship game for the third time in four years. Yet another Broncos victory prompted Rick Reilly to assess Elway's place in NFL history. The Broncos would lose to San Francisco, 55–10, in the Super Bowl—Elway's third loss in the big game—but their quarterback still belonged in the league's pantheon.

By Rick Reilly

Okay, we'll soon be starting construction on the Joe Montana wing of the Pro Football Hall of Fame. But while we're at it, maybe somebody should start dusting off a shelf back near the broom closet for Denver Bronco quarterback John Elway. What else are we going to do with Elway? He continues doing his impression of the Energizer bunny. He keeps going and going and going....

He especially keeps going to Super Bowls. In fact, Elway will be going to his third in four years, thanks to his jaw-dropping performance Sunday at Denver's Mile High Stadium, where he beat the Cleveland Browns with a contortionist's throws and a cat burglar's feet, 37–21, to win the AFC title.

All known methods of burying this guy have failed, and the Browns know it better than anyone. You can't do it with statistics. Elway was ranked ninth among AFC passers this season, but first in wins. You can't do it with pressure. Elway said he felt "suffocated" this year by the expectations of Denver's fans and media, then went out and exceeded those expectations. You can't do it with blitzes and shoots and stunting defensive ends. He will only dance away from them and then carve the defense into an armchair doily.

Elway answered all the criticism in the 1989 season by dancing his way to yet another Super Bowl.

One for the ages: Elway completed 20 of 36 passes for 385 yards and three touchdowns.

Maybe all that now stands between Elway and a display case in Canton is his oft-clobbered dream, his long-pined-for Super Bowl victory. Of course, what stands between him and *that* are the San Francisco 49ers....

Two serious Super Bowl whippings in 1987 and '88 left some Bronco fans hoping that their team would lose against the Browns and save them the angst. "Why don't those people go hide in their closets?" Elway said before the game. "They're taking the easy way out. If we lose, we lose, but I'd hate to be stuck in a closet."

And that was only one of the juicy tidbits that preceded the latest renewal of what has become a wonderfully testy rivalry. Forget the game—people were talking about The Box, The Sox and, of course, The Ox.

The Ox was Cleveland coach Bud Carson's and owner Art Modell's worry that there wasn't enough oxygen at Mile High Stadium. Team doctors had advised that the less exposure the Browns had to Denver's thin air, the better it would be for them. So new NFL commissioner Paul Tagliabue agreed to let the Browns arrive one day before the game instead of the required two....

Modell decided to further tweak his hosts by refusing to sit in Denver's visiting owner's luxury box, calling it a "disgrace" and choosing to pay $5,000 to rent a different luxury box....

Then came The Sox. Denver receiver Vance Johnson painted a Frank-buster symbol on his practice hose—the jersey number 31, worn by Browns cornerback Frank Minnifield, with a slash through it...."He's like a bad rash," said Denver receiver Michael Young, who would have a career day, with two catches for 123 yards and a touchdown. "He holds more than any defensive back in the league...."

[Denver took a 24–7 lead in the third quarter, but Cleveland's Bernie Kosar directed two drives to bring his team to within three points.]

"I could just see it," said Elway, conjuring up a twist on past meetings between these two teams. "The Drive. The Fumble. The Comeback."

Wrong. Meet The Throw. On third-and-10 from his own 43, in the most important Denver drive of the day, with the momentum seeping out of the stadium, Elway spun away from the relentless Cleveland rush—if Montana had Elway's offensive line, he would be a life insurance salesman by now—fled to his left, chose not to visit with Browns defensive end Al (Bubba) Baker, who was eager to speak with him, saw only one receiver even remotely lonely and threw the ball on the run, across his body, at least 25 yards east-to-west and another 20 north-to-south, over the hungry digits of—guess who?—Minnifield and into the hands of Johnson. Two plays later, Elway connected with Winder for a 39-yard touchdown, on which Winder eluded two tacklers, one of whom was—you guessed it—Minnifield.

Kosar was intercepted on each of the Browns' next two possessions, [Denver kicker David] Treadwell added two more field goals, of 34 and 31 yards, and the Broncos started to think about making their dinner reservations at Antoine's in New Orleans.

"You tell me how he does it," said Denver quarterbacks coach Mike Shanahan of Elway's performance. "How can he be running left, his toe pointed the wrong way, and still throw it the opposite direction and drop it with perfect touch? *That's coaching.*"

Baker couldn't quite believe Elway, either.

"I was all over him, and he throws an out-of-the-shoulder-socket pass all the way across the field! All day he was outrunning guys with 4.4 and 4.5 speed! If he keeps this up, I'm going to have to be a John Elway fan."

Stand in line. "What a magnificent performance," said Modell. "It's equal to Unitas, Namath, Graham—anyone over the years."

People say he doesn't win the big ones, but if Mr. and Mrs. Montana had never had Little Joe, wouldn't Elway have been the quarterback of the 1980s?...

Johnson sox-ed it to Browns defenders with a game-high seven catches for 91 yards.

DRIVEN

After finishing the regular season with a 12—4 record and the fifth AFC West title of Elway's career, the Broncos ran into Houston and its hot quarterback Warren Moon in the divisional playoffs. Moon staked the Oilers to a 21—6 lead with touchdown passes on his first three drives, and Houston led 24—16 midway through the fourth quarter. The inimitable Rick Reilly recorded Elway's 19th career fourth-quarter comeback.

By Rick Reilly

Nobody likes to look into the valley of death and spit as much as John Elway. Nobody is better when the dogs are at his cuffs, the barn is burning and the rent hasn't been paid. No wonder Elway owns three car dealerships in the greater Denver area. Who runs a better year-end closeout drive than he? Eighteen times in his nine-year career he had gathered up his outrageous nerve, magic cleats and nuclear right arm and taken the Denver Broncos from behind in the fourth quarter to win. But surely not this time. Not again.

For one thing, the Houston Oilers had just punted the Broncos into a cozy little corner at their own two-yard line. For another, there was only 2:07 left in regulation, and Houston's murderous and underrated defense was going to blitz everybody but the Gatorade boy. There were 98 yards to go, no timeouts to go it in, and Elway was ready to be fitted for a stretcher. At one point in the fourth quarter of this semifinal playoff game in Denver, he was so out of breath that one of his linemen told Elway that his teammates were having difficulty understanding him in the huddle. Yeah, he had pulled off The Drive, the 98-yard wonder in Cleveland in the 1986 AFC Championship Game, but this situation here was downright unthinkable. One thing about miracles: They don't Xerox well.

Elway proved definitively that, when he is involved, miracles *can* be Xeroxed.

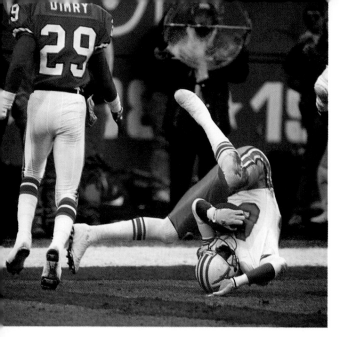

Haywood Jeffires made this touchdown grab to help Houston build a 21–6 lead.

Mile High Stadium was a giant woofer. On the Denver sideline, Bronco backup quarterback Gary Kubiak was resigning himself to permanent goathood. He had bobbled a perfectly good snap and ruined an extra-point attempt in the first quarter. Now, as the minutes ticked down, Denver was behind by that one botched hold, 24–23. "I was standing there thinking, I've got to live all year knowing I messed up that PAT," Kubiak said.

As Elway got ready to drag himself back onto the field one more time, Kubiak yanked on his arm. "Pick me up, Wood," Kubiak said. In sportsese, "pick me up" means "save my bacon." Wood is what Kubiak calls Elway, Wood being short for Elwood, Kubiak's handle for Elway. To Elway, Kubiak was always Koob. Drafted the same year—Elway the shiny first pick in '83, Kubiak the 197th—Kubiak always knew what the score was in Denver. He would sweep up after Elway's parade. Still, they became roommates and best friends. In Elway's first few tumultuous years in Denver, the years when he felt hounded, confused and ready to quit, nobody dealt out more hang-in-theres than the Texas farm kid, Kubiak.

But there was more than just bacon to be saved this time, and they both knew it. Elway knew that Kubiak was going to retire after the season. Maybe nobody but Elway cared about the retirement of a lifetime understudy. Here was a guy who had spent his best years behind one of the most durable and celebrated quarterbacks in history....

"As I was walking out there," Elway said, "I was thinking, We can't let Koob end his career on that bobbled snap."

Some great things are done for history. Some for glory. Some for country, family, God, self. But once in a while, in the dark of a chill January afternoon, great things are done in the name of a roomie....

Now it was fourth-and-10, still 65 yards

from a touchdown, only 59 ticks to go, Denver's third fourth-and-the-season down of the day. Coronary specialists turned on their beepers. Every alley Elway looked down, there was a guy standing with a gun. The crowd at Mile High Stadium was beside itself. On the scoreboard, in 15-foot-high letters, read a simple comment: THIS IS TENSE.

But who is better in a furnace than Elway? He took the shotgun snap, stepped up in the pocket, eluded the fingers of [defensive end

In the process of passing his way to victory, Elway salvaged an old friend's dignity.

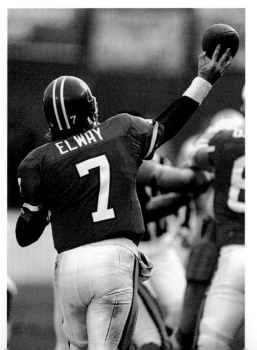

William] Fuller and darted forward as if he might run. Ahead of him were two Johnsons. The one in orange was Denver receiver Vance. The one in blue was Houston cornerback Richard. One knew what Elway would do. One didn't. Richard ran toward Elway, refusing to give up another maddening first-down scramble. Vance took off madly toward the sideline. Elway tossed the ball on the run. "Not my prettiest pass," he said, "but it got there." When it did, Vance turned upfield and saw a very pretty sight—open pasture. Forty-four yards later, Denver had a first down at the Houston 21....

One play later, [kicker David] Treadwell trotted onto the field for a 28-yard field goal try with 16 seconds remaining that could make Son of The Drive a legend. Off came Wood. On came Koob to hold. Unfortunately, as the snap came toward Kubiak, it was low, dangerously low. It's funny how sports can be so wonderfully symmetrical. A guy asking to be bailed out can suddenly bail himself out. Kubiak did not catch it so much as he smothered it, trapped it. As Treadwell started forward with his right leg, Kubiak somehow righted the ball. Treadwell double-clutched, Kubiak spun the laces, and the ball went screaming off, obviously unhappy but nonetheless above the crossbar and through the uprights. Somebody call Sotheby's. Works of art can be copied. Denver 26, Houston 24....

WRITER'S BLOCK

The Kansas City Chiefs arrived for a late-season game in Denver without having won at Mile High Stadium in ten years. Chiefs coach Marty Schottenheimer was oh for six at Denver, dating back to his days as coach of the Browns, and new Kansas City quarterback Joe Montana had lost the only two Mile High appearances of his career. Rick Telander revealed how Elway and the Broncos kept those streaks, as well as Denver's '93 playoff hopes, alive.

By Rick Telander

With 12 minutes left in the Kansas City Chiefs–Denver Broncos game at Mile High Stadium on Sunday, sportswriter Reggie Rivers burst through the left side of the Chiefs' line and blocked Bryan Barker's punt. The play set up Bronco quarterback John Elway's 25th career fourth-quarter game-winning drive and took participatory journalism into a new realm.

Rivers the scribe (his weekly sports column appears in a dozen newspapers) doubles as a third-year special teams player and reserve running back for the Broncos, and this was clearly the most important career move of his life. Not only did his block give the ball to Denver at the Chiefs' 11-yard line—three plays later Elway would throw a short touchdown pass to tight end Shannon Sharpe, giving the Broncos a 24–21 lead en route to a 27–21 victory—but it also provided Rivers with fodder for this weekend's column.

"I blocked that ball with my hands," the writer said in the locker room afterward. "I think the man across from me, Bennie Thompson, thought I was trying to hold him up, so he released wide. He probably thought he beat me." The ball rocketed backward off Rivers's hand, then Barker inexplicably swatted it toward his own end zone before the Chiefs' Todd McNair grabbed it and was tackled at his 11-yard line for a 47-yard loss. The play resulted in

Elway engineered his 25th fourth-quarter comeback, outduelling fellow legend Joe Montana.

**The Denver defense kept the Chiefs' Marcus
Allen pretty much bottled up all day.**

last two minutes and the patented Elway
Drive to Victory. The brief game-winning
drive against the AFC West–leading Chiefs
was the first for Elway in the year 1 A.D.
(after Dan), and it was sweet for two reasons.
One, it showed that Elway could work his
come-from-behind magic under easygoing
first-year coach Wade Phillips; and two, it
"silenced the critics who said I couldn't do
this, couldn't do that," said Elway.

Just what "this" and "that" are is unclear,
though the answer undoubtedly has something to do with the fact that Elway has gone
to the Super Bowl three times without winning, and that even his "touch" passes sometimes leave sinkholes in his receivers' chests.
It is Elway's desire to be appreciated for
being the great tactical quarterback that he
is, not just as an "athlete" running around in
a dither and hurling last-second, cross-field
missiles for improbable and ultimately irrel-
evant wins. Indeed, the 33-year-old Elway is
thriving as never before, in Phillips's West
Coast offense, an attack that allows the quarterback to mix runs and passes in a creative
fashion, much as Elway did in the offense he
steered at Stanford in 1982 under guru Jim
Fassel, who is now Denver's offensive coordinator. Elway's 22 touchdown passes are the
most in the AFC this year, and they equal his
previous high for a season. But above all he

a net gain of some 80 yards in field position
for the Broncos, as well as a mighty swing in
momentum, and the thoughtful Rivers considered this after his shower. "I should get
that as rushing yards, don't you think?" he
said politely to the assembled fellow writers.

Absolutely, we all agreed. But then Elway
should get a Purple Heart for the 10 years he
spent directing the conservative attack of
former Bronco coach Dan Reeves, taking a
whupping while all of Denver waited for the

is overjoyed to be free of Reeves's heavy yoke. "We're going to open it up from Play One," he crowed at spring minicamp....

[The Broncos and Chiefs traded scores through much of the game, with Kansas City in front 21–17 after three quarters.]

With just over three minutes gone in the final period, came the blocked punt by Rivers, and suddenly Elway was looking at the go-ahead score. The 6' 2'', 230-pound Sharpe, sculpted like a park statue but agile as a tumbler, promptly beat safety Doug Terry on an out pattern into the right side of the end zone....

The Broncos made it 27–21 eight minutes later when Jason Elam drilled a 53-yard field goal....

There was, of course, one last chance for the Chiefs' delicate genius to work his craft. With 2:26 left to play and no timeouts, [Joe] Montana took over at his own 20. But ... Montana's final fourth-down pass fell incomplete.

"It was too much to ask of Montana," Phillips said with a shrug in the jubilant Denver locker room. "It would have been hard even for John Elway to do it." But not impossible.

"I'd much rather have *him* in that situation,"

Sharpe caught 10 passes for 65 yards and was on the receiving end of three Elway TD tosses.

Elway said of Montana. "Especially with us up by six." Then he grinned. "But if it were just a field goal you needed, *I'd* rather be in there. You never think anything's out of reach."

Certainly not a punt. Journalist Rivers, the punt blocker, continued his discourse on his intertwined careers, saying that it was his viewing of Dustin Hoffman and Robert Redford in *All the President's Men* when he was a freshman in high school that made him want to become a newspaper guy....

And now he can investigate his own role in the continuing saga of John Elway. It's a good story, and the title's a no-brainer.

Writer's Block, of course.

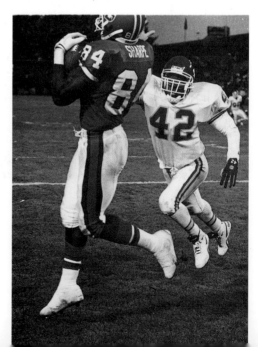

DIRE IN DENVER

The Broncos began 1994 with four straight losses under second-year head coach Wade Phillips. Sports Illustrated's Peter King traveled to Denver's next game, a matchup with division rival Seattle, to find out what was wrong.

By Peter King

...Of all the nutty things to happen to the Broncos this season, none has been nuttier than this: Elway, the Hall of Fame shoo-in, has the best supporting cast he's ever had on offense, and until Sunday, Denver was winless. A 16–9 victory over the Seahawks was salve for the wounded Broncos, but Denver is still 1–4 with a harrowing stretch of division contenders—the Kansas City Chiefs, the San Diego Chargers and the Cleveland Browns—looming the next three weeks. Amazingly, the defense carried the Broncos in Seattle, but the offense continued to be mystifyingly inept. For example, Elway, the $4.7 million-a-year quarterback and his frustrated $2.6 million-a-year receiver, Anthony Miller, did not connect on a single pass....

The pressure to reverse this season's downward spiral has fallen squarely on three men: Elway, [head coach Wade] Phillips and Bronco owner Pat Bowlen.

THE QUARTERBACK Elway lost his customary cool momentarily during a conversation

The win over Seattle got the 500-pound gorilla off the backs of Elway and the Broncos.

a few days before the game against the Sea-hawks. How in the world, he was asked, could Denver be 0–4? "Look," he replied, "I make no personnel decisions. People think, well, this is John Elway's team, and that means it's John Elway's fault. I don't make any decisions. I'm a cog in the machine...."

Elway gutted out the win in Seattle, banging his right thumb on a Seahawk helmet on the second series of the game and playing with a bad bruise the rest of the day. His 15-for-29, 146-yard day was far off his standard, but it did the job. "That wasn't a monkey on our back," he said. "It was a 500-pound gorilla. Now I don't have to wake up to the clock radio telling me about the 0–4 Broncos."

Yet Elway and [offensive coordinator Jim] Fassel still have some explaining to do. Why spend a mint on Miller and send him on pass routes to nowhere? Elway didn't throw to Miller for the first 26 minutes of the Seat-tle game and wound up passing to him only five times in 29 attempts on the day. After the game Miller was frustrated. "I'm the person who caught 84 passes last year, and now I've caught 12 in five games," he said....

THE COACH ... Phillips knows that the ax is being sharpened—and it's his head on the block. Bowlen is not a patient man. "I refuse to give a vote of confidence," the owner said last week. "I'm not here to judge how a guy

coaches. I'm here to judge wins and losses...."

The biggest knock on Phillips is that he and [Personnel Director Bob] Ferguson spent too much money on offense and not enough on defense. He disagrees. "I think you can put a good defense together with less talent than you can on offense," he says. "You can play winning defense with not particularly great players who play with intensity and play well together."

Phillips pulled the right strings on Sunday, sending linebacker Mike Croel into the Seattle backfield for six tackles and three quarterback pressures. The defense gave Denver some teeth. It will need that bite until the offense starts scoring four touchdowns a game.

THE OWNER ... The Broncos are now snug up against the salary cap, which means they will have to chop some payroll in the off-sea-son to sign the defensive help they need. Worse, they don't have a pick in next April's draft until the fourth round. The only way they will obtain immediate defensive help will be to buy it on the free-agent market....

By not adding a couple of veteran defensive players—Richard Dent or Rickey Jack-son or Leonard Marshall—Denver made it almost mandatory that Elway put big numbers on the board every Sunday....

Denver had better hope that Elway still has lots of heroic football left in him. He'll need it to save both Phillips's job and Denver's season.

August 7, 1995

ONE MORE DRIVE

Sports Illustrated's Gerry Callahan profiled Elway as the veteran quarterback welcomed a new coach and a new offense to Denver— changes he hoped would finally bring him a Super Bowl ring.

By Gerry Callahan

He first appeared in the thin air of Mile High Stadium 12 years ago, a gift to Denver from the football gods. He had the arm, the teeth, the hair, the attitude and the aura. He was the first player taken in the '83 draft, but he made the Baltimore Colts trade him and the rest of the country hate him. Still, when he lined up under center, everyone pulled up a chair to watch. He was only the most exciting young quarterback in NFL history.

John Elway could throw, run and do magic tricks in the final minutes of games. He could sell cars, shoot par and tell his grandchildren that he stood up George Steinbrenner when the Boss tried to persuade him to give up football for a career as the New York Yankees' right-fielder. He could do just about anything, on or off the field, and if you were a card-carrying member of the anti-Elway crowd, there was only one consolation: He couldn't do it forever.

From the beginning, it was obvious that the one thing Elway wouldn't do better than everyone else was age. How could he? He took too many hits and relied too much on his unparalleled physical skills. There were too many demands on his time and too much pressure to carry the team on his shoulders. The autograph pests and hotel-lobby hustlers came at him harder than the outside linebackers ever did—tugging, grabbing, everyone looking for a piece of Elway.

How long could he put up with it? Sooner or later, just being John Elway would take its toll. "With John, I don't worry about the physical aspect of the game," says Mike Shanahan, Elway's new head coach and the Broncos' third in four years. "I think the mental part is what will eventually drive him out of the game. There's just such a demand on him that he's going to reach a

Those who considered Elway too reckless to survive have had to concede his astonishing durability.

Elway entered the '95 season with a fragile left knee but high hopes for another title shot.

terback it's like dying and going to heaven," he says of the offense that Shanahan brought with him from the San Francisco 49ers, where he was the offensive coordinator for the past two seasons. "I feel like I'm starting over again."

On June 28, Elway made a generation of football fans feel old when he celebrated his 35th birthday. Jack Elway's kid is now old enough to be president. His face looks worn and weather-beaten; touches of gray show through his sandy, surfer-boy hair. He is beyond MTV age and well into his VH1 years. For the first time in his career he is the oldest player on the Broncos and the fourth-oldest starting quarterback in the NFL. He walks like he just rode a horse in from Kansas, but then he strode into the league with a kind of Walter Brennan hobble. "I've always had a bad walk," he says, smiling. "I know I don't have the quickness I once did, but I'm still learning, still getting better. I honestly don't feel like I'm done yet...."

During Elway's 12 years in Denver there has never been an offensive star among the supporting cast, a Rice to his Montana, a Pippen to his Jordan. And Elway has never had an offensive line like the one that keeps

point where it's no longer fun to play."

The bad news for unforgiving [Colts] fans is that he hasn't gotten to that point yet. He has a new coach, a solid new cast of veteran teammates and an intricate new offense that makes him feel like a kid again. "For a quar-

Dan Marino safe in Miami. Elway has rushed 596 times in his career for 2,670 yards and been sacked 416 times. Marino, a draftmate, has been sacked just 178 times. On the list of great quarterbacks in NFL history, there aren't many who have had to scrape themselves off the turf as often as Elway.

Perhaps the most amazing part of all his legendary fourth-quarter comebacks was that Elway invariably was limping into and out of the huddle when he performed them. For all his remarkable physical gifts, his durability might be the most impressive part of the package. Elway has missed 17 of a possible 186 starts. He frequently plays hurt because he doesn't know any other way. "And unlike some quarterbacks, he never looks over at the sidelines or up in the stands when he takes a hit, trying to elicit sympathy," says seven-year veteran Hugh Millen, entering his second year as Elway's backup. "He knows it's part of the game. Everyone gets hit. He just gets up and goes back to the huddle. Believe me, his teammates notice that."

Team doctors do, too. Elway runs through his medical history without a hint of self-pity, the way a pro golfer reviews a bad round. "Nine surgeries," he says. "Both shoulders, elbow, foot and five on the knee." Before you offer to throw him over your shoulder and Medi-Vac him to the cafeteria for lunch, Elway adds, "But only one was a real operation—the one on my knee in high school. The rest were just cleanups." He makes it sound like all it took was a little soap and water....

The team might prefer to see him settle into the pocket and not scramble so often this season. Shanahan's new offense calls for quicker drops and shorter pass routes, which, aside from trying to keep Elway in one piece, will give him more opportunity to dispel the notion that he is all bombs and bravado, a macho gunslinger in an increasingly high-tech game....

"I don't know if John will admit it, but he's really excited about this season," says [tight end Shannon] Sharpe. "He thinks this team can win a championship, and he knows this might be his last chance to get one...."

He is still the man with everything, the Golden Boy with the golden touch, but he is getting greedy in his old age. He wants one more thing before he limps away forever.

"There's such a stigma about the guys who've never won it," says Elway. "It's not fair, but I know that's the way it is. I would love another chance. You could say that's why I'm here. I want to retire a champion."

The most exciting young quarterback in NFL history is growing old. Time *is* running out on John Elway. You might want to pull up a chair one last time. This could be good.

THE MOUNTAINTOP

THE MOUNTAINTOP

By Michael Silver

Of all the truths John Elway held to be self-evident, knowing when to quit was the one he felt most sure of. He'd talk it over with his parents, run it by his kids, have a candlelight dinner with his wife, Janet, and make the transition into retirement without regret.

Then, on the night of Aug. 4, 1997, he felt a sensation he'd never anticipated. Wincing in pain after rupturing his right biceps tendon during an exhibition game against the Miami Dolphins in Mexico City, Elway realized it could all be over.

No más? For Roberto Duran, maybe, but not for Elway. Forget The Drive or the remarkable 41 fourth-quarter, game-winning marches he had engineered to that point. This might have been Elway's most amazing comeback of all. No one can recall an NFL quarterback resuming his career successfully after rupturing his biceps. Elway, unbelievably, said the injury made him *better*, which simply serves to prove, in the words of *SI's* Austin Murphy, that for Elway the biceps "is nothing more than extraneous gristle."

It was as if the football gods were giving Elway one more chance, perhaps to make up for the cruel ending they had levied against him the previous January. After adapting to Broncos coach Mike Shanahan's San Francisco–style offense, in 1996 Elway produced perhaps his greatest regular season, earning his fifth Pro Bowl berth and finishing second to the Green Bay Packers' Brett Favre in the MVP voting. The two were on track to settle the debate

Elway's brilliant play enabled the Broncos to jump out to a blazing 9–1 start in the '97 season.

JOHN ELWAY

in the Super Bowl, but the top-seeded Broncos, huge favorites in their opening playoff game against the Jacksonville Jaguars, an expansion franchise in its second year, failed to stop Jags quarterback Mark Brunell and absorbed a stunning 30–27 defeat. Once again, Elway was reminded how difficult it is to reach the top.

Now, in '97, more determined than ever to return to the Super Bowl, Elway shook off his biceps tear and led the Broncos to a 9–1 record. Then Denver lost three of its next five games, straggled into the playoffs as a wild-card and faced a seemingly impossible task. Since the advent of the wild-card round in 1978, 116 teams had been forced to play an extra postseason game. Only one, the 1980 Oakland Raiders, had won the Super Bowl.

But this was a different Broncos team from the ones Elway had carried in the past. For starters there was Terrell Davis, running behind a quick, feisty offensive line, to provide balance. There were impact players on defense as well, such as linebacker John Mobley and defensive end Neil Smith. And Shanahan's cool, brainy leadership kept the Broncos from folding.

The Broncos hosted the Jaguars in a playoff rematch, and Denver ran wild, rolling up 310 rushing yards in a 42–17 victory. Then the Broncos went to Kansas City and, on the strength of Elway's second fourth-quarter comeback drive of the season, pulled out a 14–10 victory over the top-seeded Chiefs. A week later, deep into the AFC title game at Pittsburgh, Elway broke from the huddle, told his most reliable target, All-Pro tight end Shannon Sharpe, "Get open," and fired a fastball into his chest for the game-clinching first down.

Earlier in the season, Elway had issued the stunning declaration that Davis had displaced him as the team leader. Nice try, John. Everyone in the Broncos' locker room knew the tenor of the team's effort would be determined largely by the attitude and play of No. 7. Indeed, though Davis's heroic, MVP performance was critical, it was a defiant, acrobatic leap by Elway on a run near the goal line that energized the Broncos on their way to the 31–24 victory that ended the AFC's 13-game losing streak.

Elway's triumph captured the heart of the nation and elevated him to the rarefied realm of the alltime NFL greats. Suddenly, all those disappointing defeats from years past didn't seem so significant. "It means the other three Super Bowls are all erased now," John said after the game as he hugged his wife, Janet. "Those were the ultimate losses. But this is the ultimate win."

Elway engineered yet another fourth-quarter comeback in Denver's playoff win over Kansas City.

December 30, 1996

A GREAT RUN

In 1996, after Elway had led the Broncos to the NFL's best record at 13—3, Rick Reilly offered this classic profile of the 36-year-old superstar, who was playing some of the best football of his 14-year career.

By Rick Reilly

When you order up the statue of the greatest quarterback of the last 20 years, make sure you get the sock right. It has to be pulled all the way down, preferably with a defensive end's fingernail still in it. Give the right shoe a flat tire, and show the jersey yanked off one shoulder pad, the work of a blitzing linebacker who thought he had himself an appearance on the next *NFL's Greatest Hits* video but instead got only a fleeting handful of orange-and-blue Denver Broncos nylon. It's true, you know. John Elway has spent more time on the job having his padding adjusted than Pamela Anderson Lee.

While you're at it, see if the sculptor can put in a hint of the bulges of tape and a knee brace underneath the legs of the pants, and of the limp that made Elway walk like John Wayne in high heels yet vanished when he took off sprinting, needing six yards and somehow always getting six yards and an inch.

Try to show the jaw-dropping power of that right arm, the one that shredded receivers' gloves and knocked the wind out of strong men. Elway threw the worst screen passes in NFL history, but he could get the football to you at rush hour in the middle of Penn Station from a hoagie stand across the street.

Make the eyes huge, wide as beer coasters, like the eyes of somebody witnessing a disaster—which, come to think of it, Elway usually was. Seems like every time you looked up from your nachos, it was fourth-and-10, the Denver pass protection had collapsed like a bad soufflé, and he was starring in another cliffhanger: *John Elway and the Pocket of Doom.*

By the end of the '96 season Elway had become the No. 5 NFL quarterback alltime in rushing.

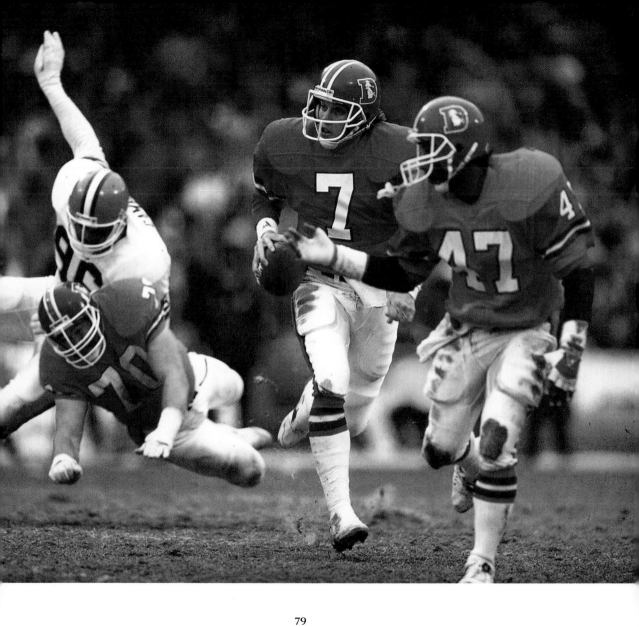

In January 1987 Elway scrambled to his first AFC title with an overtime win over the Browns.

Keep it honest, too. Show those dark circles under the eyes, and the crow's feet—more crow's feet than any 36-year-old man should have, carved there by 14 years of trying to win with small-fry linemen, cement-footed receivers and witness-protection-program running backs. Everybody wants to talk about Super Bowls, but forget Super Bowls for a second and try this: Punch rewind on your time machine and put Elway behind all of Joe Montana's lines in San Francisco and Montana behind all of Elway's lines in Denver. Nothing much changes in San Francisco, but by the age of 28 Montana is either dead or selling life insurance.

That is the thing, really. John Elway never

had a Guy McIntyre. John Elway never had a Jerry Rice. John Elway had a whole lot of guys who are now waiting tables.

So far in Elway's career, his offensive linemen and wide receivers have been voted to the Pro Bowl a combined six times. In Dan Marino's 14 seasons, Miami Dolphins offensive linemen and wide receivers have been selected to the Pro Bowl 30 times. More than any athlete since Wilt Chamberlain on the Philadelphia and San Francisco Warriors of the late 1950s and early '60s, Elway has had to play at a superb level game after game, year after year, to make his team a winner. Though usually surrounded by a human rummage sale, Elway has won more games as a starter than any other quarterback in NFL history (126). It's the equivalent of carving Mount Rushmore with a spoon or composing Beethoven's Ninth on a kazoo.

But Elway's career has been about more than just winning. It has been about escaping defeat a half page from the end of the novel, leaping over pits of fire with the microdot hidden in his cigarette lighter. On first down Elway was "pretty average," his Stanford coach Paul Wiggin once said. But when the elementary school kids are being held hostage and the detonator reads 00:03, whom would you rather have clipping the wires than Elway? He may be the only quarterback in history who could stand on his own two-yard line, trailing by five with less than two minutes to play, no timeouts left, windchill -5°, and cause the opposing coach to mutter, "We're in trouble...."

It's weird, but Elway will be a first-ballot Hall of Famer partly because of all the things he does wrong. For instance, he doesn't stand up tall in the pocket. Years ago his father, Jack, a longtime college coach who's now the director of pro scouting for the Broncos, told him, "Always be ready to run." And so John sets up with his knees bent, constantly bouncing on the balls of his feet, more than ready to leave a sinking ship. Nobody else is close to his nine seasons with

at least 3,000 yards passing and 200 rushing.

He routinely throws across the field, making the one pass quarterbacks are taught never to try. Elway does it from one sideline to the other and from one 20-yard line to the other. It's a wonderful way to run up your interception total, but not only have the Denver coaches not told him to stop, they also once put such a pass in their playbook—scramble right, turn suddenly and throw 40 yards downfield and 40 cross-field. "Sometimes in practice that play would come up on one of my snaps," says Elway's old backup Gary Kubiak, now the Broncos' offensive coordinator. "I'd always pretend to slip just before I threw. What could I do? I mean, nobody else in the *world* can make that throw."

And under a heavy rush Elway turns his back to the line of scrimmage, a cardinal sin. He feels the hit on his body and spins away from the pressure, like the Houston Rockets' Hakeem Olajuwon, even if that sends him running away from his receivers, blockers and sanity. And yet the spin has been to him what the Aston Martin was to James Bond: his signature means of escape....

Some of the joy gradually went out of the game for Elway after he turned pro in 1983 and found himself playing under a coach whom he would grow to hate, Dan Reeves. It sounds crazy, but it wasn't until four years

Despite the pounding he took through the years, Elway has missed only 10 games to injury.

ago, after Reeves was fired, that the Broncos built their offense around Elway. For 12 years Denver's offense reflected Reeves's conservative philosophy. Reeves's idea of letting his hair down was to allow a running back to go out for a pass once a month....

Since the split with Reeves, Elway's passing yards per season have increased 23%, his touchdowns have gone up 47% and his interceptions have been reduced by 24%. But the most definitive stat of Elway's career remains the record 40 times he has brought the Broncos from behind or from a tie in the fourth quarter and won the game. The stat not only shows Elway's two-sizes-too-big

heart but also shows how deep a ditch he often has found himself in. "There's a reason he was always making those come-from-behind victories," says [tight end Shannon] Sharpe. "We were always *behind*. What Reeves did, it was like making Picasso paint with a spray can.…"

O.K., O.K., the Super Bowl thing. The world loves to point to the bad endings, the Broncos' three crushing Super Bowl losses, but the fact that Elway has been to three is preposterous in itself. "Nobody but John Elway could've taken those three teams to the Super Bowl," says Shanahan. To this day Elway has never watched a replay of any of his Super Bowls … and no wonder. Denver was thumped by the Giants 39–20 in 1987, by the Washington Redskins 42–10 in '88 and by the 49ers 55–10 in '90. "It hurts too much," he says....

This year—this gleeful year for Elway—is different. For the first time he may end up not taking a team to the Super Bowl but going with one. He is handing off to the NFL's leading rusher, Terrell Davis. He is throwing to two Pro Bowl sets of hands, those of Sharpe and wideout Anthony Miller, two men who, remarkably, are actually bigger than Eddie Gaedel. He is setting up behind one of the finest lines in football, anchored by Pro Bowl tackle Gary Zimmerman. It must take all of Elway's willpower not to come to the line grinning. "This is so great now," he says, beaming. "Before, I'd go into a game just dreading it."

With his quiver finally full of arrows, Elway is having his sharpest all-around season. Admit it, none of us thought he would be a good old quarterback. We figured that howitzer arm or those Energizer legs would be gone by now, and his sandlot shtick would be over. But he's more of a technician than anybody thought. He can be Montana if he

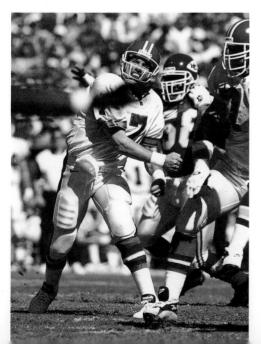

wants—checking options 1, 2 and 3 and then dumping—or he can still be 23 years old, the human escape clause, leaving a trail of panting defensive ends in his wake and then throwing the ball from here to February. If he is not the league's MVP—most versatile, most volatile, most valuable player—then they should melt the trophy into a hubcap....

Elway's goal has always been to be "the best quarterback ever to play the game." How's he doing? "I'm playing better football than I've ever played. Maybe I'll never get there statistically because of my first 10 years, but if I can be the best now, the best this year, *one* of the best to ever play, that would work too...."

If Denver wins it all, [Elway's wife] Janet thinks John will retire. John grins that lopsided grin of his and says, "I'd love to have to cross that bridge. Oh, man, I'd *love* it."

When he's finally gone, goose bumps will be at an alltime low. The other day, as Elway was getting ready to head to Mile High, he asked his seven-year-old son, Jack, if he was going to come to the game and see his dad play. Jack began listing all the things he needed to do that day: play soccer, play basketball, play Nintendo, etc.

Elway sighed and said, "You know, Dad's not going to be playing football forever. You ought to come and watch while you can."

Sounds like excellent advice.

January 12, 1998

ARMS RACE

In one of his best seasons ever, at age 37, Elway led Denver to a 12—4 record in 1997. But the Broncos still finished one game behind rival Kansas City in the AFC West, which meant they would begin their Super Bowl journey in the steerage class that is the wild-card berth. No matter, Denver easily dispatched Jacksonville—avenging a bitter playoff loss in the previous year— to set up a second-round tilt with the Chiefs in Kansas City. Sports Illustrated's Michael Silver was there.

By Michael Silver

He bounded onto the field with a spring in his step, as elated as the 76,965 fans at Arrowhead Stadium were deflated. John Elway, one of the more dignified competitors of his generation, had succumbed to the sadist within. His Denver Broncos, just having repelled the Kansas City Chiefs' last-ditch fourth-down pass into the end zone, held a 14–10 lead with 12 seconds remaining in their AFC divisional playoff game. All Elway had to do was handle one snap and take a knee, and Denver would advance to the AFC Championship Game in Pittsburgh against the Steelers.

This wasn't as gripping as the Drive in 1987 or any of Elway's other famous comebacks, but to him it was just as sweet. "There's nothing I love more than going on the road and shutting up an opposing crowd," Elway had said three days before Sunday's victory—the Broncos' first road playoff triumph in nearly 11 years....

After a season of handing the ball to All-Pro halfback Terrell Davis and trying to protect leads, the Comeback Kid is alive. In Pittsburgh, Elway, 37, will face the new wonder: [25-year-old] Kordell Stewart, who got an up-close view of Elway while playing quarterback at Colorado and who has referred to him as the Man....

Yet another of Elway's patented fourth-quarter drives sank the Chiefs in the '97 playoffs.

[Kansas City coach Marty] Schottenheimer has made the playoffs 11 times in 13 seasons as a head coach but has yet to reach the Super Bowl; he came closest when his Cleveland Browns reached the 1986 and '87 AFC title games, but both times Elway thwarted the Browns. Elway entered Sunday's game holding a 13–8 career edge over Schottenheimer, with seven fourth-quarter comebacks.

Think Schottenheimer gets a kick out of the rivalry? Anyone who spent time with the Chiefs last week can set you straight. Schottenheimer is big on rhetoric and notorious for going over the top in his speeches during meetings, but he hit a new plateau. Among his biting comments to K.C. players was a facetious slap at Elway's bowlegged gait: "I want you to take that crook leg of his and straighten it...."

Against the Chiefs, Elway was sacked only once, while connecting on 10 of 19 passes for 170 yards.... A play on the second snap of the fourth quarter ... sparked the game-winning drive. Kansas City had just taken a 10–7 lead. On third-and-five from the Chiefs' 44, Elway, working from the shotgun formation, read a zone blitz in which no defender rotated to the left flat. Wideout Ed McCaffrey ran a right-to-left crossing route from the right slot. Elway delivered the ball perfectly, and the slow-footed McCaffrey chugged down the left sideline to the one, setting up a second touchdown run by Davis, who finished with 101 yards on 25 carries.

Because ... Denver never trailed in the fourth quarter of its previous 13 victories ... Elway's comeback skills had been dormant. "I like to think it's like riding a bike, that you never lose the ability to come back," he said last Thursday. "Playing with a lead is totally different. There's a fine line between not losing your aggressiveness and making dumb plays that let them back in the game...."

As he walked into the chilly Kansas City night to join his teammates on buses ... Elway was besieged by autograph seekers. He happily obliged those wearing Broncos colors, but he had no time for Chiefs fans.... A few steps from the bus, a freckle-faced youngster wearing a sweatshirt bearing Schottenheimer's likeness tapped Elway on the shoulder. Elway whirled around.

"Please, John," the boy begged.

For a split second Elway appeared sympathetic. Then his face turned cold. "Sorry, buddy," Elway said. He spun and boarded the bus, crook leg and all.

STEPPIN' UP

Denver lost three of its final six regular-season games in '97, including a 35–24 defeat to Pittsburgh on Dec. 7 in which the Steelers' up-and-coming quarterback, Kordell Stewart, outshined his veteran counterpart on the Broncos. In the return match for the AFC championship, however, the old man got the last word, and Sports Illustrated's Austin Murphy heard it loud and clear.

By Austin Murphy

Six days before the AFC Championship Game, Denver Broncos cornerback Ray Crockett read the game plan and experienced a moment of clarity. He then wrote in the dog-eared spiral notebook he uses as a journal, *Me against Yancey Thigpen. If I win this battle, we win the game.*

Thigpen, the Pittsburgh Steelers' Pro Bowl wide receiver, had tortured the Broncos on Dec. 7, making three touchdown catches in a 35–24 victory in which upstart Steelers quarterback Kordell Stewart seemed to be asking his 37-year-old counterpart, John Elway, *Aren't you getting a little old for this?* The loss relegated Denver to wild-card status, making its road to the Super Bowl vastly more difficult.

That road reached a critical juncture midway through the second quarter of Sunday's AFC title game at Three Rivers Stadium. With Pittsburgh on the move, threatening to take a 21–10 lead, Stewart made the first of his several poor decisions in the game, locking in on Thigpen—even though Thigpen was smothered by Crockett and free safety Steve Atwater—and letting fly the pass on which the game turned. "Yancey did a little stutter step, and I didn't go for the stutter," recalled Crockett, who made a leaping interception in the end zone. That play set up the touchdown drive that gave the Broncos a 17–14 lead they never surrendered en route to a 24–21 win....

Elway's solid performance sent him into the Super Bowl with his strongest supporting cast ever.

You will be reminded ad nauseam over the next week and a half that the AFC has lost the Super Bowl 13 years running. You will learn that this game constitutes a homecoming for Denver running back and San Diego native Terrell Davis, who has suffered from chronic migraines—as opposed to Elway, who suffers from a chronic inability to win the NFL title game. The Broncos have been outscored 136–40 … in Elway's three Super Bowl losses. "I know we'll be huge underdogs, but ask me if I care," said Denver defensive end Neil Smith…. "No one thought we'd come this far."

That lack of faith was understandable.

Denver faltered down the stretch, dropping three of its final six regular-season games before rattling off three playoff wins. The biggest difference for the Broncos in the postseason has been a dramatic improvement in their defense, which has benefited greatly from the return to health of Smith and fellow defensive end Alfred Williams, both of whom were plagued by torn triceps this season. Williams, in fact, tore both of his.

"Oh, is that why we beat them the first time?" asked Steelers running back Jerome Bettis last Friday. "It's always something, isn't it?"

"Ask him if he noticed any difference today," riposted Smith, who bunny-hopped into the locker room after Sunday's game, so overjoyed was he to be Super Bowl–bound for the first time in his 10-year career. On Dec. 7 he was dominated by Pittsburgh right tackle Justin Strzelczyk, but on Sunday, Smith had the upper hand. For instance, with 1:43 left in the first half, he beat Strzelczyk around the corner, drawing a holding penalty that wiped out an 18-yard completion. As a result the Broncos got the ball back in the last minute before intermission and drove for the touchdown that put them up 24–14.

On the last play of the third quarter,

THE DRIVE OF A CHAMPION

Smith sacked Stewart and forced a fumble that defensive tackle Mike Lodish recovered at the Denver 41. It was Smith's third sack of the playoffs. He and Williams had two apiece in Denver's 14–10 divisional playoff win over the Kansas City Chiefs, with whom Smith spent his first nine pro seasons.

Rather than having his players sit back on defense and allow first-year starter Stewart to dissect them, as had happened a month earlier, Denver defensive coordinator Greg Robinson this time threw a far more exotic mix at the Steelers. Defensive linemen did more slanting and stunting, the better to confuse Bettis and to prevent Pittsburgh's hogs from teeing off on them. Broncos backup linebacker Glenn Cadrez came in on passing downs to "spy" Stewart, while the secondary showed a variety of looks. Don't take this the wrong way, cornerback Darrien Gordon had been told before the game, but Crockett's going to cover Yancey this time. It was Gordon who was thrice burned for touchdowns by Thigpen on Dec. 7.

"We wanted to make him beat us throwing the ball," Broncos linebacker Bill Romanowski said of Stewart, who wasn't up to it. Pittsburgh's first possession in the second half—an 11-play drive—ended with Stewart's third interception: He tried to muscle a pass to wideout Charles Johnson, who was sur-rounded by three defenders, and linebacker Allen Aldridge made the interception for another touchback. Romanowski immediately got in the quarterback's face, calling him a "dumb s‑‑‑...."

A pair of Denver's aging defensive linemen conversed nervously with two minutes left in Sunday's game. The Steelers had closed to within three points; the Broncos' offense faced third-and-six on its own 15. "Hell no, we're not going back out there," Williams said to Lodish. "Somebody's going to make a play."

The likelihood of that happening was lessened when Elway walked into the huddle and called All Thunder, a play he had made up and no one else had heard of. "So John just went down the line, saying, 'You run a go route, you run this, you run that, everybody just get open,'" said wideout Rod Smith, who led Denver receivers against Pittsburgh with six catches—all for first downs—for 87 yards.

As Shannon Sharpe broke the huddle, he asked Elway, "What should I do?"

"Just get open," Elway said impatiently.

Just get open, Sharpe repeated to himself as he jogged to the line. O.K. He ran an eight-yard hitch, gathered in Elway's bullet, broke a tackle and got 10 more yards for a first down that would enable Denver to kill the clock. The Broncos were Super Bowl–bound....

SEVEN UP

Fifteen years, 44 game-winning fourth-quarter drives, 48,669 passing yards, four AFC titles: John Elway's career had it all—except a Super Bowl ring. Indeed, he had been to the big game three times and lost all three. His legacy, it seemed, was destined to include great glories, but also the knock that he couldn't win the big one. That changed in 1998, when the football gods granted Elway a shot at redemption in Super Bowl XXXII. Michael Silver recounted the fairy tale that few believed would come true.

By Michael Silver

He spent 15 years pushing the physical limits of football, making jaws drop and decorating highlight clips with bursts of brilliance. Then, with one fearless thrust of his 37-year-old body late in the third quarter of Super Bowl XXXII, John Elway finally lifted himself and the Denver Broncos to the top. In the greatest Super Bowl ever, the pivotal moment, fittingly, belonged to one of the NFL's alltime greats.

For all the importance of coach Mike Shanahan's dazzling game plan, of running back Terrell Davis's MVP performance and of the game-ending stand by Denver's oft-slighted defense, it was Elway, with his self-described "three-inch vertical leap," who elevated himself into immortality and his franchise into the realm of champions with the Broncos' 31–24 upset of the Green Bay Packers on Sunday.

The play said everything about the defiant Broncos and their unlikely march to the title: With the game tied at 17 and Denver facing third-and-six at the Green Bay 12, Elway dropped back to pass, found no open receivers and took off down the middle of the field. He darted right and was met near the first-down marker by Packers strong safety LeRoy Butler, who ducked his head and prepared to unload on the quarterback. Elway took to the air, and Butler's hit spun him around so that he came down feet-forward as he was absorbing

With the game won, Elway enjoyed a celebratory ride off the field and into the history books.

Elway's daring third-quarter leap produced a crucial first down and inspired the Broncos.

another shot from defensive back Mike Prior.

When Elway hit the ground at the four, an adrenaline rush surged through the Broncos. Denver scored two plays later, and though the Packers came back to tie the score again, Green Bay was a depleted team fighting a losing battle against an opponent that had been recharged.... "When Elway, instead of running out of bounds, turned it up and got spun around like a helicopter, it energized us beyond belief," Denver defensive lineman Mike Lodish said after the game....

The Broncos carried a confidence into this game that belied their station as a double-digit underdog....

While the AFC's 13-year Super Bowl losing streak and Denver's 0–4 record in the big game helped convince many experts that a Green Bay blowout was inevitable, Shanahan saw no cause for panic. As early as eight days before the game, he ... [said] to one reporter, "Just between you and me, we're going to win the game. With all this hype Green Bay's getting, the whole AFC inferiority thing, how Denver has played in the Super Bowl and how the Packers played against the 49ers [in Green Bay's 23–10 NFC Championship Game victory on Jan. 11], everybody will be stroking them. It will all work in our favor, and our guys are pretty determined."

Shanahan and Elway could barely contain their excitement the evening before the Super Bowl as they reviewed the game plan in Elway's hotel room....

Shanahan was convinced he could get inside the head of Packers defensive coordinator Fritz Shurmur, who relies on the versatile Butler for frequent blitzing and run support. Shanahan believed that when Denver lined up in a slot formation—an alignment with two receivers to one side of the line and the tight end to the other—he could predict Butler's assignment based on the safety's positioning. Denver had spent the season running out of its base alignment and passing from the slot, but on this day all of its runs came from the latter formation. Green Bay never adjusted. The Broncos gained 179 yards on the ground, even though they ran for no yards in the second quarter while Davis (30 carries, 157 yards, three touchdowns for the game) sat out with blurred vision after getting kicked in the helmet during a first-quarter run. "The Packers were outcoached, pure and simple," Sharpe said....

Meanwhile, Broncos defensive coordinator Greg Robinson rattled the normally unflappable [three-time NFL MVP Brett] Favre,

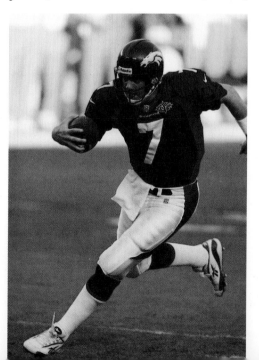

throwing blitzes at him like right-wingers flinging sex rumors at President Clinton. Favre threw for three touchdowns, including an ominous 22-yard strike to wideout Antonio Freeman on the game's first possession, but he never found his rhythm. Denver did what few observers believed it could—survive an instant Green Bay score, get away with daring Favre to beat its cornerbacks in man-to-man coverage and, unlike so many AFC patsies of recent years, win the turnover battle ... 3–2.

After Denver won the AFC title at Three Rivers Stadium, Shanahan had little trouble persuading his players that, by comparison, playing the Packers at a neutral site was no cause for a coronary....

Green Bay manufactured some incentive of its own, most of it derived from the media's focusing on Elway's quest to win a Super Bowl after three washouts.... "We've heard all about poor John Elway," defensive tackle Santana Dotson scoffed three days before the game. "We're all very touched. But, hey, that's the classic pregame story. As long as we're the focus of the postgame story, that's cool."

Sorry, Santana. History will show that this was Elway's week of glory. Sure, his stats were wimpy. He threw for only 123 yards, didn't

Elway's legs were nearly as important as his arm in the Broncos' upset victory.

complete a pass to a wideout until Ed McCaffrey's 36-yard catch-and-run midway through the third quarter and blew a chance to build on a seven-point lead by throwing an end zone interception to free safety Eugene Robinson with 11 seconds left in the third quarter. But Elway carried the day with his poise [and Denver became only the second wild-card team— the 1980 Oakland Raiders were the first—to win a Super Bowl]. "That was the ultimate win, there's no question," he said. "There have been a lot of things that go along with losing three Super Bowls and playing for 14 years and being labeled as a guy who has never been on a winning Super Bowl team."

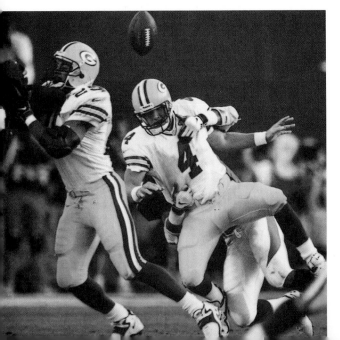

Remember how shaky Elway had looked at the beginning of his last Super Bowl appearance, against the 49ers in January 1990, when he threw his first pass into the ground and the Broncos went on to lose 55–10? After that game he and wide receiver Michael Young, now Denver's director of corporate sales, were the last players to leave the locker room. When Young asked Elway if he was O.K., Elway shook his head no. "They'll never, ever forgive me for this," he said, referring to the fans in Colorado.

This time Elway was as steady as the jets that buzzed the stadium during his introduction. He dismissed the Robinson interception from his mind immediately, and when he strutted onto the field with 3:27 left, the score tied at 24 and the ball on the Green Bay 49, he was in control and confident. "I looked at John before he took the field, and he had this huge smile on his face," Jeff Lewis, Denver's third-string quarterback, said after the game. "You could see it in his eyes; he was ready. It was one of those times you just have to stop yourself and watch the best quarterback ever do his thing."

It helped that the Broncos' offensive line, despite being the league's lightest, had worn down the Packers defenders.... Still, it was

Favre, under pressure all day, coughed the ball up on this sack by Steve Atwater (obscured).

Elway's game to pull out, a chance for the quarterback with the most victories in NFL history to win the big one, finally. Put some points on the board, have them hold up, and all would be forgiven and forgotten.

On his biggest pass of the game, Elway made a perfect delivery, throwing a quick toss to fullback Howard Griffith that went for 23 yards and gave Denver a first-and-goal at the eight with two minutes remaining. That set up Davis's winning one-yard touchdown run.... "John makes mistakes; he is human after all," Broncos receiver Rod Smith would say later. "But you never see fear in his eyes. He's like a linebacker with a good arm."

Even when that golden right arm was being used to hoist a few beers, Elway was zeroed in on the upcoming game. On the first two nights after the Broncos arrived in San Diego, Elway, Lewis and Bubby Brister, Denver's No. 2 quarterback, commandeered a limousine to take them around town. At several bars Elway elected to remain in the limo, alone with his thoughts. "One time I stayed in the car with him," Lewis said, "and he was so focused, it was amazing. He said, 'I can't wait for this game. Before the other Super Bowls, I really didn't grasp how big they were. But I've never been this ready for a game in my life.'"

He was so loose that his wife, Janet, was unnerved. "I keep waiting for him to snap at me, to end a conversation abruptly, but he's still so loose and happy," she said four days before the game. "That's not like him; he usually saves his happiness for afterward...."

It's a measure of how far Denver has come that Elway, who once had to carry his team, didn't have to be spectacular in his finest hour. Shanahan built these Broncos to reflect his own personality—resilient, businesslike and fearless. Strong safety Tyrone Braxton, whose first-quarter interception set up Denver's second touchdown, knew the significance of the victory extended beyond the realm of Elway. "It means everything," Braxton said, "not only for this team but for the past Broncos teams, all the way back to 1960 [the year the franchise played its first season in the AFL]. We're not a city of losers anymore, and we won one for the AFC. It's been a long, hard road for all of us."

Later Shanahan celebrated with [Denver owner Pat] Bowlen in [a] limo while his 18-year-old son, Kyle, discussed how relaxed his father had been in the hours before the game. "He was ultramellow," [Kyle said.] "We were sitting in his hotel room watching *White Men Can't Jump*, and he was laughing his head off."

Funny how things work out. White men can't jump? Don't try telling that to the Packers—not after Elway's leap into history.

PHOTO CREDITS